CONTENTS

Jill Barker is hereby identified as author of this work in accordance with Section 77 of the Copyright, Designs and Patents Act 1988

YORK PRESS
322 Old Brompton Road, London SW5 9JH

PEARSON EDUCATION LIMITED
Edinburgh Gate, Harlow,
Essex CM20 2JE, United Kingdom
Associated companies, branches and representatives throughout the world

First published 1999
Second impression 2000

ISBN 0-582-41459-8

Designed by Vicki Pacey
Phototypeset by Gem Graphics, Trenance, Mawgan Porth, Cornwall
Colour reproduction and film output by Spectrum Colour
Produced by Pearson Education China Limited, Hong Kong

PART ONE

INTRODUCTION

HOW TO STUDY A PLAY

Studying on your own requires self-discipline and a carefully thought-out work plan in order to be effective. Allow yourself enough time to read the entire text of the play through more than once.

- Drama is a special kind of writing (the technical term is 'genre') because it needs a performance in a theatre to arrive at a clear interpretation of its meaning. Try to imagine that you are a member of the audience when reading the play. Think about how it could be presented on the stage. It will help you to form imaginative ideas if you can see as many live and filmed versions as possible.

- Drama is always about conflict of some sort (which may be below the surface, or within the mind of a character). Identify the conflicts in the play and you will be close to identifying the large ideas or themes which bind all the parts together.

- Make careful notes on themes, character, plot and any sub-plots of the play. Be sure to include your own ideas at this stage, and think about similarities to other literary works you have read – this will make your responses more original and personal.

- Why do you like or dislike the characters in the play? How do your feelings towards them develop and change?

- Playwrights find non-realistic ways of allowing an audience to see into the minds and motives of their characters, for example soliloquy, asides or musical cues to emotion. Consider how such dramatic devices are used in the play you are studying.

- Think of the playwright writing the play. Why were these particular arrangements of events, characters and speeches chosen?

- Cite exact sources for all quotations, whether from the text itself or from critical commentaries. Wherever possible find your own examples from the play to back up your opinions.

- Always express your ideas in your own words.

This York Note offers an introduction to *Doctor Faustus* and cannot substitute for close reading of the text and the study of secondary sources.

When *Doctor Faustus* was performed by Edward Alleyn's company of players in the 1590s, a frisson of fear ran through the audience and the actors. Rumour has it that an additional, unidentified 'actor' had appeared on the stage amongst the devils that Faustus had conjured. Since then many audiences and actors have feared (superstitiously, perhaps) that Faustus's necromancy might really work: that theatre and reality could blend together, and the pretend devils become real. Alleyn himself took to wearing an ostentatiously large cross when playing the title role.

This reaction to *Doctor Faustus* makes sense if we see the play as the sixteenth-century equivalent of a horror movie. We know how easily we can voluntarily allow our emotions to be carried away – however briefly – with the idea that the monsters of the cinema might be real. When we walk home with our hearts beating faster and look fearfully down dark alleys, we are playing with the power of fictional representation to give us a special kind of thrill. Christopher Marlowe in his way, and without the benefit of cinematic effects, went very close to the edge of acceptability when he chose to play with the threat of damnation because many in his audience believed that hell existed, and that eternal damnation was a very real possibility for anyone who failed to repent of their sins before they died. Perhaps the worst aspect of hell for an ordinary person was that it opened up the speculative imagination. Whatever it was, it was worse than life, and in the 1580s and 1590s, when public torture was a standard form of punishment for criminals, that could have suggested frightful extremes.

If *Doctor Faustus* merely offered cheap titillation it would have been superseded long ago. However, it additionally contains stirring and memorable lines of poetry; theatrical moments, including ridiculous slapstick comedy; profound human pity; and an intellectual challenge to us all.

Speaking of Marlowe's poetic skill, Ben Jonson famously used the phrase 'Marlowe's mighty line' to describe his invention of **blank verse**: a strongly rhythmic, regular unrhymed line in **iambic pentameter** which is usually (but not invariably) **end-stopped**. This later became the basis of Shakespearean blank verse, but Marlowe's form was less flexible, with line-ends more clearly marked by both syntax and meaning, thus generating an effect of sinewy strength. Within the context of the experimental poetic forms of the 1570s and 1580s (see Literary Background) it brought a sense of security, confidence and power, while avoiding the jingling effect of **ballad rhythms** or the domination of **rhyming**. Marlowe handled **polysyllables** with breathtaking ease, while the beat of the line carried speeches forward in a way that was appropriate and necessary in the popular theatre.

Perhaps hardest to spot when reading the play are the opportunities for spectacular visual effects. The arrival of the Deadly Sins and the grotesque and/or tempting visions offer wide opportunities for a theatre director to put on a stunning show. Even in Christopher Marlowe's day the devil could be performed as a juggler or a fire-eater, or be accompanied by that popular (though risky) effect on the Elizabethan stage: explosions of gunpowder. The slapstick comedy is not just for show: it has some point when it involves attacking pretentiousness in various forms, by dropping a servant into a pond or by stealing the Pope's banquet. These scenes are frequently left out of performances of the play, and probably were not even written by Marlowe. Scholars have tended to see the knockabout scenes as empty and inartistic, but modern criticism is more inclined to see them as a functional part of the whole. Logically, there is certainly space for this **low comedy** as a **parody** of Faustus's own pride and his stupidity in making a bad bargain: in exchange for his soul, he has gained nothing more than a satirist's trivial trickery. It is the foolish comedy that shows us Faustus as something of an idiot, for all his great learning. However, we are brought to pity this man who hoped to become something more than human by trading his soul for superhuman knowledge. He thought he could 'beat the system' through his own intellectual powers, but is trapped by a logical **paradox**. The dynamic of the plot combines with the dignity of the poetry to manoeuvre us away from any possible sense of self-righteousness or superiority, and towards sympathy.

It is in this that the intellectual challenge lies: the play presses a need to decide what counts as totally unforgivable behaviour. The conclusion, famously, seems both to question God's judgement and to support it. It is up to the reader or audience to decide whether *Doctor Faustus* is fundamentally an atheistic play or a religious play. Hence the aim of this Note is not to try to convince you of one position or the other, but to show where some of the evidence lies. You will need to search for further evidence in the text yourself, and form an opinion based on that evidence.

To construct *Doctor Faustus*, Marlowe used many of the conventions of the medieval **Morality Play**. This popular form, a variety of **allegory**, narrated the gradual education of its hero into an understanding of the difference between right and wrong. The hero invariably came to the conclusion of the play a sadder, wiser and better man. ('Man' is most commonly the case, though these **mankind figures** were female in a very few cases.) Marlowe modified this traditional form by fitting it to the German story of a scholar/magician called Johann Faustus. Although the Faustus story had some slight basis in historical truth, wild stories of his deeds had been exaggerated and embroidered upon until they reached semi-miraculous proportions.

Marlowe's radical conclusion is a **tragic** version of the Morality Play, for instead of achieving the mankind figure's pious maturity, Faustus descends to a gloriously theatrical eternal damnation. *Doctor Faustus* continues to attract audiences for several reasons: clearly it can be a stunningly good show, filled with grotesque costumes and weird special effects; it also forms a fascinating link between medieval theatre and the Shakespearean stage without being in any sense primitive; and finally, the debate about the existence of God is of perennial interest.

PART TWO

SUMMARIES & COMMENTARIES

Two early printed versions of *Doctor Faustus* exist, each with some claims to being seen as closer to the 'original' version written by Christopher Marlowe, probably with the help of a collaborator, as was common practice in writing for the theatre in the sixteenth century. No original copy of the play direct from Marlowe's own hand has ever been found, and the two printed versions date from some years after Marlowe's death in 1593.

The earliest edition, first published in 1604 and referred to by scholars as the 'A-text', is substantially shorter than the later 'B-text' of 1616, but also contains material which the B-text omits. It is known that extra material was written for the play in 1602, and either (or both) of the printed texts may contain these alterations and additions. Scholars, beginning with W.W. Greg in his introduction to *Marlowe's Doctor Faustus 1604–1616: Parallel Texts* (Clarendon, 1950), have suggested that the following chronology plausibly explains what happened to Christopher Marlowe's play. Greg believes that the play was written in 1592, possibly in collaboration with Samuel Rowley. He sees the 1604 **quarto** as a reconstruction of actual performances from memory. This reconstruction has also been cut short in places and supplemented with comic scenes, thus creating a new acting version which was more accessible to 'vulgar' audiences, and more easily performed by a small touring company. Greg believes that the 1616 text, on the other hand, went through substantial changes, having been put together by an editor who had access to the author's drafts in the form of a damaged and partially illegible manuscript, and also to a copy of the 1604 edition. This editor may also have made alterations and cuts, adding scenes of slapstick comedy to recapture a dwindling audience, and changing references to God in obedience to the Jacobean ban on the naming of God on stage (the 1606 Act of Abuses). This argument would make the 1604 quarto (used here) the closer to Christopher Marlowe's concept of the work. Clearly neither text gives us a direct link with Marlowe's original ideas, but in a way this does not matter given that most plays of the period were collaborative efforts, and neither authors nor audiences expected the kind of stylistic homogeneity that many literary critics have since lauded. Most scholars, including Roma Gill and Bevington & Rasmussen (the editors of authoritative recent editions), believe that Marlowe had an anonymous collaborator right from the start, who wrote the comic, rough-and-tumble scenes.

We can study either version of the play, and some editions combine the two. W.W. Greg's 1950 edition of the parallel texts enables the reader to see precisely where the differences occur. The Revels Plays edition by D.M. Bevington & Eric Rasmussen (Manchester University Press, 1993) also prints both texts, but in sequence; the introduction to their edition contains a detailed discussion of the A- and B-texts, and their relation to each other. Most recent modern versions of *Doctor Faustus*, such as the New Mermaids edition by Roma Gill (A & C Black/W.W. Norton, second edition 1989, reprinted 1994), have the best of both worlds by following the A-text as the primary source, but printing the extra scenes as an appendix. Gill divides the play into 'scenes' and 'choruses', avoiding the anachronistic five-act structure which some editors adopt.

This Note is based on Roma Gill's New Mermaids edition. For readers who are using other versions, the following summary of the differences between Gill's system of dividing into scenes, and that of Bevington & Rasmussen, may be helpful. Reasonably enough, Gill's Scenes 1, 2, 3 and 4 appear as Act I, Scenes 1, 2, 3 and 4. Bevington & Rasmussen begin their Act II at the beginning of Gill's Scene 5, which they divide into Scene 1 (lines 1–176) and Scene 3 (lines 176–end). Between these two, however, they place Gill's Scene 6, which they re-designate Act II, Scene 2. With Gill's Chorus 2, Bevington & Rasmussen begin Act III (Chorus), and then proceed logically enough with Scene 7 as Act III, Scene 1 and Scene 8 as Act III, Scene 2. Gill's Chorus 3 begins Bevington & Rasmussen's Act IV; Scenes 9 and 10 are conflated as Act IV, Scene 1, and Scene 11 becomes Act IV, Scene 2. Bevington & Rasmussen combine Gill's Chorus 4 with Scene 12 as Act V, Scene 1, leaving the long Scene 13 as Act V, Scene 2. The Epilogue closes the whole piece in both versions.

Roma Gill's edition, with its fluid structure in which a Prologue and Epilogue frame thirteen scenes interspersed with three Chorus speeches, recaptures the easy transitions of the pre-Shakespearean stage to which Marlowe's dramaturgy belongs.

SYNOPSIS

The story is set in Germany, where Dr John Faustus, a brilliant scholar, feels that he has reached the limits of human understanding. Desiring greater challenges and power, he contracts to sell his soul to Mephastophilis, an emissary of the Devil, in exchange for twenty-four years during which he will be given a luxurious life, magical powers and illicit knowledge of the secrets of the universe. Faustus fails to notice that the limitations on the Devil's expertise and on the time during which he can enjoy the bargain are of crucial significance. Faustus's servant, Wagner, joins in the conjuring process at a lower level of skill. In spite of some spiritual doubts, Faustus perseveres in his commitment to deny God.

Scenes of magic alternate with moments of doubt. The twenty-four years pass without a strong sense of narrative development, in a series of magic tricks of more and more dubious value: Mephastophilis supplies Faustus with intellectual, physical and theatrical pleasures, including a parade of the Seven Deadly Sins. He enables Faustus to become invisible in order to play practical jokes on the Pope. A series of slapstick shape-shifting scenes takes place, sometimes involving Faustus, sometimes servants and ostlers (Robin, Rafe, the Vintner, and the Horse-Courser).

The play ends where it began, in Wittenberg, where Faustus's last magic is to show his old friends a vision of Helen of Troy. An Old Man attempts to bring Faustus to repentance, but Faustus holds to his devilish contract. His last night on earth passes in a speech of anguish and longing, during which Faustus perceives what heaven means, but refuses (or is unable, depending on the interpretation) to turn to God. He is dragged screaming to hell.

PROLOGUE **The Chorus (a solitary speaker) explains that the subject of the play is contemporary rather than classical, and then sums up Faustus's early life, stressing his ordinary social origins, his academic success, his growing pride and his obsession with the occult**

The Chorus explains that the play to be performed is not about battles, love or heroism on the grand scale, but about an ordinary person. Faustus came from poor parents in Germany, and became a talented scholar at the University of Wittenberg. His intellectual skill led him to lose all humility, since he could defeat anyone in argument. Unfortunately, one level of pride led to another, and he became excessively ambitious. When the story proper opens, Faustus is just about to start on his study of magic.

> The Chorus functions as a curtain-raiser, attracting the audience's attention by addressing it directly, and giving some idea of the situation before the action starts. He (in Choruses 2 and 4 the Chorus is identified as Wagner) begins by announcing all the topics that the play will *not* cover. This attempt to clear away false expectations may seem confusing, as it causes the audience to notice a list of distracting ideas in rapid succession, but in fact it makes us more content when he leaves those behind to focus on simpler, practical things. The narrative that follows is clear and to-the-point, sketching the situation of the play in three lines (20–22). Characteristically, the Chorus offers a doubt about Faustus's fortunes: will they be 'good or bad' (line 8)? This we are left to discover. The Chorus's mediation between the audience and the central performance provides a sense of daily life as a theatrical event: of moral decisions as being under observation, in a way reminiscent of the well-known contemporary commonplace (or **topos**) that life is a stage performance (for example, Jaques's 'All the world's a stage' speech in Shakespeare's *As You Like It*). In this re-interpretation of the relationship between audience, presenter and action, the Chorus momentarily sees Christopher Marlowe himself as the Muse (line 6), even though the Muse was normally the (female) inspirer of the poet, and not the poet himself. Indeed, the description of the verse as 'heavenly' (line 6) suggests that the poet could be just as **hubristic** as Faustus. Commentators have

often tried to draw parallels between Faustus and Marlowe, but this is much disputed – clearly the attitudes expressed by a fictional character in a play may have some, little or no relation whatsoever to the beliefs held by the writer.

The Chorus initiates a verbal technique which features in the play and in Faustus's mind: the confusion of moral terms, especially through the use of physical images to discuss spiritual matters. Faustus is 'glutted' with learning (line 24) as if he has eaten too large a meal and now, his palate spoiled, he finds he can **metaphorically** eat to greater excess ('surfeits', line 25) if he studies black magic, which he finds unnaturally 'sweet' (line 26). The mind thus appears to be just one of the appetites.

1 **Thrasimene** the location of a battle against the Romans won by the Carthaginian statesman and general Hannibal in 217BC

2 **Mars** the Roman god of war

mate match – an odd usage, as 'mate' was frequently used to mean 'defeat'

21 **waxen wings** the Chorus is comparing Faustus **proleptically** to Icarus, a figure in classical Greek mythology whose father, Daedalus, invented feather wings held together with wax; Icarus disobeyed his father's warning and flew too close to the sun – this caused the wax to melt and Icarus to fall into the sea and drown. The Icarus myth became a popular **symbol** of over-ambition and **hubris**

SCENE 1   **Faustus lists the great authors he has read, all of whom now seem useless to him. He hopes that magic will make him godlike. He sends his servant (Wagner) to fetch Valdes and Cornelius, who are to be his tutors in black magic. While Faustus awaits them, the Good and Evil Angels briefly offer him advice, then exit. Valdes and Cornelius arrive and offer him untold wealth and power. They plan to meet for a further lesson later that evening. The scene closes with Faustus promising to go forward with studying magic**

The scene follows smoothly from the preceding speech, and begins with Faustus seated alone amongst his books. He will need to refer to these as the scene goes on. Faustus speaks, listing the discoveries and ideas of each

of the great authors he has studied, and imagines giving himself over
wholly to each field of knowledge in turn: first, theology, then philosophy
(and logic), then medicine, then law. Each discipline, however, is
superseded by another, until all seem useless to him. He gives theology a
last chance, but feels that it is logically inevitable that all human beings
must sin and so die. He turns to magic in the hope that, combined with
his intelligence, it will make him godlike and capable of transcending
mortality, which is the human condition. This is a subject in which he is
still a novice, so he sends his servant, Wagner, to fetch the magicians
Valdes and Cornelius, who can teach him how to gain power over the
spirit world.

While he is waiting, the Good Angel and the Evil Angel appear.
The Good Angel threatens Faustus with God's anger if he follows his
present course, while the Evil Angel follows by suggesting that Faustus
can achieve great earthly power. Faustus rhapsodises on the varied uses to
which he might put such magical power, including acquiring personal
wealth, winning patriotic victories for Germany, redirecting the flow of
the Rhine river, and becoming King.

Valdes and Cornelius enter and Faustus repeats his ideas to them.
They feed his expectations, promising the services of spirits in many
disguises, and eventually all three decide to continue the discussion over
a meal, after which Faustus hopes to learn enough magic to practise it
independently. The scene closes with Faustus resolving to attempt his
first experiment with magic. They leave together.

> This scene puts forward an initial understanding of Faustus's
> character and motivations. His opening speech needs to be
> considered closely, as it contains an analytic discussion of the beliefs
> which he will no longer hold, before moving on to describe what he
> really wants to achieve. Structurally, then, it is a little like the
> Chorus's technique of disposing first of what will no longer be
> relevant: a lot can be learnt by examining what Faustus disclaims
> and considering the context within which his decision is taken.

> The odd-sounding stage direction 'Enter FAUSTUS in his Study' may
> be interpreted as the Chorus drawing a curtain back to reveal the
> spectacle of Faustus at work with his books; alternatively, Faustus
> may enter by walking on with one or more volumes in his hands.

When he quotes directly from Aristotle and Justinian, this is often performed as reading aloud from the books. However, his partial quotations from the Bible are not in fact from Jerome's Vulgate Bible, so he cannot read those from the text.

Faustus is given to thinking aloud, in **soliloquy**. Whereas in the Prologue the Chorus was clearly addressing the audience, here Faustus is wrestling with a problem. He addresses himself by name, creating the impression that he has some control over what he is doing, but at times he also addresses the books as if they were people: 'Sweet *Analytics*, 'tis thou hast ravished me' (line 6). The speech could be performed on stage as an articulation of Faustus's thoughts, on which we as the audience are invisible eavesdroppers. Much more theatrically effective might be to abandon an illusion of realism and perform these solitary speeches as confiding in the audience at some points.

Faustus approaches his decision systematically, by considering the purpose of each of the intellectual disciplines, knowing that his own learning gives him sufficient background to undertake this task. First, the intellectual achievement of the Ancient Greek philosopher Aristotle is described in sensual, almost sexual terms as having 'ravished' Faustus (line 6). Mind and body are indistinguishable within this way of speaking. Each necessary Latin phrase is translated for the audience, which suggests that the play was intended for the public stage and not for private academic performance. Faustus decides that Aristotle teaches that the goal ('end') of logic is merely 'to dispute well' (line 8) – in other words, to conduct formal arguments without making errors of logic. If so, he can gain nothing further from Aristotle, because he knows how to do that already; thus he bids farewell to '*on kai me on*', a Greek phrase meaning 'being and not being'.

He then turns from philosophy to medicine, epitomised by Galen, describing the purpose of medicine as a way of making money and becoming famous. These attract him for the moment, until he considers the additional goal of achieving health: since he already has this himself, and has already achieved fame for his cures, he decides that medicine is not worth studying. He wants something more than money or fame, it would seem: something that will challenge the boundaries of what counts as human ('Yet art thou still but Faustus, and a man', line 23). Modern-day readers might see similarities here between the monster created by Frankenstein and the un-human being that Faustus wishes to create of himself – in this respect *Doctor Faustus* shares some of the qualities of the horror genre, long before its time. Faustus might also be seen as blasphemous – making people live forever and raising them from the dead describes the activities of Christ in the New Testament. Indeed, the image of Christ as a physician was a popular one in the late Middle Ages and the Early Modern period. Faustus therefore implies that he would only be a doctor if he could be the same as Christ – another way of saying that he wishes to be God, or perhaps to be some kind of equal to God. As is explained later in the play, the pride that this evinces is precisely that for which Lucifer was cast out of heaven (Scene 3, lines 65–9):

FAUSTUS

Was not that Lucifer an angel once?

MEPHASTOPHILIS

Yes Faustus, and most dearly loved of God.

FAUSTUS

How comes it then that he is prince of devils?

MEPHASTOPHILIS

O, by aspiring pride and insolence,

For which God threw him from the face of heaven.

The audience understands the **dramatic irony** with which Faustus's own fate is narrated, apparently unknown to him.

Faustus next considers the legal profession in the form of Justinian's Laws, and mentions two famous cases. To discard Justinian, Faustus adopts the traditional Christian view that material wealth is 'trash' (line 35) in comparison with spiritual things. Yet he does not see that the magic he plans to take up is substantially different from the spirituality which defines money as trivial. He thus compartmentalises his thinking, using whatever approach is most convenient at a given time but discarding it later when it becomes inconvenient to him, while apparently noticing no inconsistency. The cases he looks at can perhaps be seen as **metaphors** for Faustus's position: one of them concerns values, the other concerns inheritance from father to son – Faustus, in rejecting God, will reject the figure often called a 'father in heaven', and also reject the spiritual inheritance which Christianity has to offer.

When Faustus finally turns to Jerome's Bible he is scarcely in a mood to find anything positive in its pages. The verses he recites are incomplete – he reads despairing portions but omits the optimistic phrases that follow. Once again, he uses only that which suits his argument, for he finds nothing but sin and death in the Bible. He reasons that if 'The reward of sin is death' (line 40) and all human beings inevitably sin, then all must die. He fails to consider repentance and mercy. Turning from Latin to Italian, he comments '*Che sara, sara*' – 'What will be, shall be' (lines 47–8), a fatalistic misinterpretation of Church doctrine.

The flaws in Faustus's reasoning are obvious: this is the way in which somebody talks who has already decided on a course of action, and wishes to justify it – all commentators have noticed that he reads incomplete fragments from the Bible, for example. The speech sounds more like a ritual of farewell than an **argument**. Ironically, when Faustus rejects the achievements of past thinkers it is because they are too material and therefore petty, not seeing that his own interpretation of magic mistakes its gross materiality for a kind of spirituality. In all these cases the mind (or spirit) is only important as the means: their effects are similarly worldly to him. He fails to see the Christian message that only a virtuous life – however petty its content – will yield a non-material conclusion. In turning to black magic, Faustus does not apply to it the same tests he has applied to the other disciplines, merely exclaiming that he finds the prospect of temporal power hugely exciting. He is also enchanted by the mathematical properties of incantation. 'All things that move between the quiet poles' (line 56) includes only the earth, and Faustus's assumption that his own imagination will suffice to make him a god is yet to be tested.

Having reached his decision, Faustus sends his servant to fetch
Valdes and Cornelius, who will instruct him in magic. He sees no
inconsistency in aiming to be a god and requiring human assistance
in the project: the incongruity is driven home by the leaden-
sounding word 'plod' (line 69) to describe his progress. In this
moment of expectation, the two Angels appear, who engage in a
brief dialogue in which they attempt to persuade Faustus to follow
diametrically opposed courses of action. The Angels are best seen as
genuine visitations, though there are some scholars who prefer to
interpret them as manifestations of Faustus's own inner struggle –
as **allegories** of his divided mental processes. For example, James
Smith says 'a large measure of the action takes place not so much
between beings as within a single one of them, Faustus himself; of
whom the Good and the Evil Angel, for example, are parts'
(*Marlowe's Dr Faustus* (1939), reprinted in John Jump (ed.),
Marlowe: Doctor Faustus (Macmillan, 1969), p. 51). As in a
traditional **Morality Play**, Faustus appears to hear only the last
speaker, in this case the Evil Angel, who promises him power over
the elements. Carried away with visions of worldly possibilities,
Faustus next moves into one of the many richly poetic speeches of
the play (lines 79–89):

> Shall I make spirits fetch me what I please,
> Resolve me of all ambiguities,
> Perform what desperate enterprise I will?
> I'll have them fly to India for gold,
> Ransack the ocean for orient pearl,
> And search all corners of the new found world
> For pleasant fruits and princely delicates.
> I'll have them read me strange philosophy,
> And tell the secrets of all foreign kings;
> I'll have them wall all Germany with brass,
> And make swift Rhine circle fair Wittenberg

The persistent use of liquid 'l' sounds in the repeated words 'all' and
'I'll' makes the list of Faustus's ambitions sound charming and
benign. The 'l' sounds are especially languorous in combination
with other consonants, for example in 'resolve', 'gold', 'world', 'fly',

'pleasant'. We can hear how much sensual pleasure Faustus invests in his imaginative capacities and in the worlds of novelty that his mind can open to him. Combining historical fact with fantasy in a manner characteristic of Marlowe, this passage goes on to build images far beyond the capacity of theatrical special effects – however, one might feel that the words are enough without the reality of the things to substantiate them. After all, the members of an audience in a theatre make do with a representation of ideas – we do not see 'the real thing' happening, yet we are content to enjoy the play as presented. Faustus, however, is not content. Even the sumptuous language with which he seduces himself into becoming a magician is not enough on its own: he wants 'the real thing'. As the play progresses, the question arises whether Faustus does in fact receive the things that he believes magic will provide.

As if conjured, his instructors arrive at the very moment he mentions their names. He explains that the main point of his plan is to be famous throughout Europe for his feats. Valdes and Cornelius see magic as a kind of slave-owning condition: they promise Faustus that the spells they will teach him will make devils and spirits perform his commands, in particular by shape-shifting into the forms of the people and animals that Faustus wishes to see. These spirits will have no choice because the power of the magic spells compels them to obey. Where Faustus was interested in what the spirits could bring him, the more experienced magicians are interested first in what the spirits themselves might mimic, and only as an afterthought in the riches they might capture. Valdes introduces two themes which will reappear. With 'Shadowing more beauty in their airy brows / Than in the white breasts of the Queen of Love' (lines 128–9), he hints at the possibility that Faustus might conjure up women for his pleasure, a possibility that is realised with the appearance of Helen of Troy in Scene 12. Secondly, with 'If learned Faustus will be resolute' (line 133), Valdes foretells the need for strong determination on Faustus's part. In choosing to use and live by magic, Faustus is not choosing an easy path. Indeed, it is a matter of life and death, as he recognises in his choice of closing words: 'This night I'll conjure, though I die therefore' (line 166) is a casually colloquial oath which carries the extra significance that Faustus will die not just in the simple sense, but in the Christian sense of an eternal spiritual death which comes of turning against God and 'eternal life'.

5 **Aristotle** Ancient Greek philosopher and scientist. His writings and ways of thinking were much studied through the Middle Ages and the Early Modern period

7 ***Bene disserere est finis logices*** (Latin) 'to argue well is the goal of logic'. Faustus translates this himself in the following line

12 ***on kai me on*** a transliteration of an Ancient Greek phrase meaning 'being and not being' – a traditional topic for philosophical debate

13 ***ubi desinit philosophus, ibi incipit medicus*** (Latin) 'where the philosopher ends, there the physician begins'

16 ***Summum bonum medicinae sanitas*** (Latin) 'the ultimate good of medicine is health'. Faustus translates this in the next line

27 **Justinian** Roman Emperor (from AD527 to 565) and jurist. His codification of Roman law was used as a textbook by law students

28–9 ***Si una eademque res legatur duobus, / Alter rem alter valorem rei*** (Latin) 'if one and the same thing is left to two people, one should receive the thing, the other should receive the value of the thing'

31 ***Exhereditare filium non potest pater nisi ...*** (Latin) 'a father may not disinherit his son unless ...'

38 **Jerome** during the fourth century AD, the monk and scholar St Jerome (Eusebius Sophronius Hieronymus) produced the Vulgate (Latin) version of the Bible which was widely used through the Middle Ages. The Old Testament was originally written in Hebrew and the New Testament in Greek – Latin was a more widely accessible language than either of these

39 ***Stipendium peccati mors est*** (Latin) 'the payment for sin is death' (from Romans 6:23)

41 ***Si peccasse negamus, fallimur, et nulla est in nobis veritas*** (Latin) 'we deceive ourselves if we say that we do not sin, and there is no truth in us' (from I John 1:8)

56 **poles** the North and South Poles of the earth

63 **to gain a deity** to become a god

113 **Gravelled** out-argued

116 **Musaeus** mythical bardic poet

117 **cunning** knowledgeable

Agrippa Cornelius Agrippa (1486–1535) was renowned as a magician who could raise spirits ('shadows') of the dead

121 **Indian Moors** indigenous South Americans, colonised and treated as inferior by the Spanish

Spanish lords not necessarily nobility, but powerful overlords to be obeyed

125 **Almaine rutters** German cavalry

129 **the Queen of Love** Venus, sometimes associated with Venice (as in the following line)

130 **argosies** ships carrying valuable goods; the word is suggestive of *Argo* (the name of the ship in which Jason searched for the golden fleece in Greek mythology), a reference which is picked up in the following line

131 **golden fleece** valuables brought to Spain from the American colonies

132 **old Philip** King Philip II of Spain (1527–98), son of Emperor Charles V, who appears in Scene 9 (see also Chronology)

139 **Enriched with tongues** competent in foreign languages

well seen in minerals having a knowledge of chemistry, especially of ores and minerals

143 **the Delphian oracle** the oracle of Apollo at Delphi, which was supposed to be able to foretell the future

154 **Bacon** and **Abanus** supposed practitioners of black magic

155 **Hebrew Psalter** the Psalms in Hebrew

SCENE 2   **Two scholars ask Wagner where Faustus is. After some joking, he tells them, and they express fear that Faustus will be damned**

Scene 2 opens with two of Faustus's old acquaintances wondering where he is nowadays. Faustus's servant, Wagner, chances by and teases them with a **parody** of scholarly discourse – he postpones answering their question by using literal interpretations of their remarks and playful manipulations of logic and theology. When Wagner eventually tells them that Faustus is at that moment dining with Valdes and Cornelius, the scholars immediately realise that he is learning the art of black magic. They resolve to try against the odds to save him.

The first sentence of this scene generates a sense that Faustus has changed his habits recently: people who used to enjoy his company no longer see him. We see some of the warmth, friendship and community that he has lost by taking up black magic. In contrast with these nameless scholars' concern, the greed and selfishness of Valdes and Cornelius looks meretricious.

This is the first of the **low comedy** scenes. It does not advance the plot or give the audience much in the way of new information. In Wagner, the play offers a sophisticated version of the traditional comic servant, combining the **Morality Play** Vice (see Literary Background) with aspects of the 'running slave' motif from Roman comedy. Wagner **parodies** scholarly discourse, turning ordinary conversation into a jokey form of logical **argument** Each remark by the scholars is analysed by Wagner for its logical accuracy as formal argument. Terms such as 'follows' (line 7) indicate **syllogistic** argument, while 'witness' (line 13) evokes legal terminology, and discussions of the natural body suggest theology and philosophy. Wagner amuses himself by playing verbally with a variety of ways of understanding the world. Thus we see that the servant is very competent in his master's areas of skill.

The scene can be regarded as serving two purposes: it suggests how petty scholarship is, and it provides the audience with some variety and relaxation between the intensities of Scenes 1 and 3.

1 **wont** accustomed

2 ***sic probo*** (Latin) 'thus I prove (it)' – this phrase normally signalled the conclusion of a chain of reasoning demonstrating an unlikely or difficult proposition

3 **boy** servant (of any age, not necessarily a child)

8 **Go to, sirra** colloquial phrase roughly equivalent to 'don't mess me around' or, in this case, 'talk sensibly, you cheeky person'

10 **licentiates** graduates
   stand upon't to base one position on another fact

18–19 ***corpus naturale*** (Latin) natural body

19 ***mobile*** (Latin) moveable

21 **phlegmatic** one of the medieval **humours** used to categorise the personality

21–2 **to lechery – to love I would say** Wagner first speaks the truth about himself, then adjusts the negative term 'lechery' to a euphemism. This verbal

behaviour is characteristic of the **Morality Play** Vice (see Literary
Background)

25 **precisian** a Puritan. Wagner's closing mock-blessing imitates the Puritans'
conventions of elaborately pious speech (see also Historical Background)

SCENE 3 **Faustus conjures up a devil named Mephastophilis. They
discuss Mephastophilis's master, Lucifer, and the terms of
the bargain by which Faustus will sell his soul in exchange
for magical powers. They arrange to meet later to
conclude the bargain**

It is night, and Faustus enters alone, having learned in the interim
how to make magic. His conjuring words, a lengthy Latin speech, are
followed by the entrance of a devil with a repulsive appearance. Faustus
exercises his power over Mephastophilis, sending him away to return
in a more congenial shape. **Satirically**, he suggests that the most
appropriate shape is that of a holy monk. Faustus gloats over his new-
found powers, but when he orders Mephastophilis to do his bidding, the
latter disabuses him, explaining that he is really answerable to his
master, Lucifer, and can only do Faustus's bidding if Lucifer consents.
Faustus claims to be uninterested in discussions of the soul, on the
grounds that there is no such place as hell, and asks Mephastophilis about
Lucifer. Mephastophilis briefly reminds us of the story in which Lucifer
was once the chief of the angels but, suffering from the sin of Pride, tried
to rival God and was banished from heaven forever. Faustus proposes a
contract with Mephastophilis's master: that in exchange for Faustus's
soul, Lucifer should give him twenty-four years of living 'in all
voluptuousness', with Mephastophilis at his command. Mephastophilis
leaves to consult his master, while Faustus enthuses about the feats he
might achieve.

Faustus's opening **soliloquy** picks up the **imagery** of the **elements**
with which the play is steeped to create a sinister and threatening
atmosphere, beginning with an invocation to darkness (lines 1–4).
This he sees as the time when the earth dominates over the sky.
The earth is the **element** connected with the body, as opposed to
the air (connected with the soul), and so it suggests both physicality
in general and those things that have turned from God (see Themes

regarding the body/soul binary). For practical purposes, this view sees night as a time when it is appropriate to call up a devil, for his power is strongest when the sky (that is, heaven) is overshadowed by the earth. Earth is also what God is said to have made into human beings, and earth (or 'dust') is what the body returns to in a funeral service. The soul in Christian theology is completely insubstantial and so a different matter. (Note the distinction between 'spirit' and 'soul' in *Doctor Faustus*, since Christopher Marlowe uses 'spirit' to refer exclusively to devilish beings.) Contradicting Faustus's disbelief in hell later in the scene, Mephastophilis memorably answers Faustus's questions (lines 74–7):

FAUSTUS

Where are you damned?

MEPHASTOPHILIS

In hell.

FAUSTUS

How comes it then that thou art out of hell?

MEPHASTOPHILIS

Why this is hell, nor am I out of it.

Faustus fails to learn from his friendly devil's advice, and (with unintentional **irony**) advises him to practise a masculine and specifically human strength: 'manly fortitude' (line 86) – in other words the strength of will that a human being possesses in and of himself. By contrast, the accepted Christian view is that any strength of will the individual may display derives directly from God.

Faustus's conjuring and his lengthy Latin speech of invocation should be genuinely solemn and impressive: a theatrically chilling moment. The audience is filled with suspense as it waits to find out whether or not the spirit will appear, and in what form. The appearance is not immediate: at one point Faustus actually asks in Latin 'Why do you delay?' (*'Quid tu moraris?'*, line 20). The spirit's intolerably ugly appearance could be represented in various ways, using the skills of the make-up and costume team: it need not appear in human form at all – a dragon is an appropriate possibility for a devil. Alternatively, the devil's appearance and Faustus's words 'Thou art too ugly' (line 25) could be played for laughs, with a conventionally dowdy individual as Mephastophilis's ugly first shape.

In conversation, Faustus seems to derive rich enjoyment from playing with moral contradictions. He calls his conjuring 'heavenly words', and punningly claims that there is 'virtue' in them (line 28). He is so convinced of his own cleverness that he makes several fundamental mistakes during his childish gloating. Firstly, he fails to understand the significance of the fact that he does not have total power over Mephastophilis – in fact, he has no power at all, except that which Lucifer is prepared to give him. In the first flush of his excitement, Faustus believes that this permitted power is the same as the godlike omnipotence that he seeks. Like any purchaser, he needs to take time to think through the details of the contract, but in his eagerness he forgets the skill in logic which has previously stood him in good stead. He decides that, because his 'conjuring speeches' (line 46) brought Mephastophilis to appear, then any argument over power is a quibble. This is a mistake, for Mephastophilis goes on to explain that it is not the magic tricks but Faustus's spiritual condition which brought him forth (lines 47–55). It seems that Faustus's elaborate incantations and diagrams were all in fact unnecessary, and that Valdes and Cornelius were probably charlatans. Faustus's response, in which he pledges himself to the prince of hell (lines 56–8), is off the point, for in that case he has only substituted one master for another, and is no closer to becoming a god himself than he ever was. Furthermore, the feats that Faustus plans to ask of Mephastophilis (lines 105–12) are feats which defy aspects of the *physical* world, such as distance or the strength of materials: a bridge will make the sea negligible; political power will follow; he will be able to command life and death. In short, it is engineering and its consequences for political power that interest Faustus in the speech that closes this scene. It is significant that he does not plan to control metaphysical categories such as time, for this presumably is in God's control rather than Lucifer's (God, after all, controls eternity). It is time, too, which makes a boundary around Faustus's contract – a boundary which Faustus takes for granted (the play's treatment of time is discussed in Critical Approaches).

When Faustus devises his own contract of sale, it may be argued that he does not believe that he possesses such a thing as a soul, nor that hell exists – he is thus exchanging something worthless (the soul) for something he sees as valuable (twenty-four years of physical pleasures). The exchange could be seen as an extreme kind of gamble: if he is right, he wins the pleasures and power for nothing, but if not, he loses everything in the absolute sense. Nicholas Brooke has argued that Faustus believes that he can force the contract to work for him, and create himself as a new kind of God by sheer effort of will (see Critical History).

1 **the gloomy shadow of the earth** night

2 **Orion** a constellation of stars

4 **welkin** sky

pitchy breath blackness; also, the smell of burning tar

6 **hest** command (short for 'behest')

8 **Jehovah** Hebrew and Old Testament name for God

11–12 **Figures of every adjunct to the heavens, / And characters of signs and erring stars** astrological details

16–23 ***Sint mihi ... nobis dicatus Mephastophilis*** in a Latin speech which **parodies** the rhythms of the church service, Faustus calls on numerous devils by name, and calls on Mephastophilis to appear. Roma Gill translates this passage: 'May the gods of Acheron look favourably upon me. Away with the spirit of the three-fold Jehovah. Welcome, spirits of fire, air, water, and earth. We ask you favour, O Prince of the East, Belzebub, the monarch of burning hell, and Demogorgon, that Mephastophilis may appear and rise. Why do you delay? By Jehovah, Gehenna, and the holy water which I now sprinkle, and the sign of the cross which I now form, and by our vows, may Mephastophilis himself now rise, compelled to obey us'

28 **virtue** a drug's efficacy or potency; goodness. In this sense, the 'virtue' or power of Faustus's charm is, **paradoxically**, not at all 'virtuous' because it functions for an evil goal – this is an example of Faustus's verbal wit

35 ***Quin redis, Mephastophilis, fratris imagine!*** (Latin) 'Why do you not return, Mephastophilis, in the image of a friar?'

47 **the cause, but yet *per accidens*** logic distinguishes between two kinds of cause for actions: the fundamental cause, and the immediate (or accidental) manifestation of that fundamental cause. Faustus's spells are only the outward sign of his spiritual condition, and it is his condition rather than the spells which have really brought Mephastophilis to him

60 **For he confounds hell in Elysium** Faustus sees hell as a superstition, equivalent to the Ancient Greeks' belief that the dead had a continued existence in the Elysian Fields

61 **His ghost be with the old philosophers** Faustus insists that anything that remains of him after his death might share existence with the pre-Christian thinkers of the ancient world. He avoids the word 'soul', using 'ghost' instead

62 **vain** empty, meaningless

86 **manly** not just 'masculine', but also 'human'

92 **So he will spare him four and twenty years** provided that Lucifer will let Faustus live for twenty-four years

101 **resolve me of thy master's mind** give me a firm statement of Lucifer's decision

109 **continent to Spain** joined to Spain, as one continent

114 **I'll live in speculation of this art** I'll spend my time thinking about conjuring

SCENE 4 With the assistance of two devils, Wagner persuades a character described as 'Clown' to become his servant

Wagner meets a 'clown' in an unnamed place, probably the street. He offers the clown food, lavish clothing and money if the latter will become his servant. When the clown hesitates, Wagner calls up two devils, Baliol and Belcher, who terrify him into agreeing. Wagner offers to teach him how to perform shape-shifting tricks, and the deal is settled.

This scene of **low comedy** means rather more than it seems to on the surface. The humour arises from the robust attitude of the 'clown' – a term which here means a stupid person, possibly something of a country bumpkin figure, and apparently also unemployed, ragged, and hungry. In spite of his physical destitution, Clown is alert and pragmatic – he is capable of defending himself verbally even though he is uneducated, and of detecting that there is a sinister side to Wagner's offers. We are invited to join in laughter, in part at Clown's misfortune and ignorance (for example, when he mispronounces the devils' names), but also at the incongruity of an uneducated person who is capable of putting up an argument against Wagner's persuasions. There is scope in the scene for the comedian playing Clown to include comic movements (when he is humiliated and chased around the stage by the devils) and to seem crudely lecherous in his reaction to the devils and to the shape-shifting suggestion. Humour also occurs in the word-play, for instance when Clown puns on the word 'familiar': he answers Wagner's threat that lice will become 'familiars' (devils) by saying that they are already 'familiar' (intimate) since they cover his body. Some of the humour involves slightly sniggering sexual innuendo when Clown imagines being turned into a flea in order to be closer to women.

In structure the scene involves striking a bargain, and so mimics the preceding scene where Faustus negotiates terms with Mephastophilis. Here, it is Clown who takes Faustus's role in the discussion, wondering what he will get in exchange for giving up his liberty, while Wagner takes on the function of the tempter who offers magical powers and luxury (at an appropriately trivial level). If Faustus is represented by a country bumpkin, that implies a negative comment on his own status, and on his final decision. Clown finally consents to follow Wagner out of fear of Baliol and Belcher, not because his objections are satisfied. The scene makes it clear that Faustus is behaving like the clown, and that he will not gain any worthwhile power from the bargain but only worthless and insubstantial fripperies. Furthermore, Clown's employment is as Wagner's servant, implying a parallel in which Faustus is becoming merely a servant of Lucifer, and not the omnipotent master he plans to be.

2 **Zounds** an oath (corruption of 'God's wounds')
3 **pickadevants** fashionably cut goatee beards; Clown is playing on the use of the word 'boy' (which can mean 'child' as well as 'servant')
4 **comings in** income
5 **goings out** expenses; Clown puns on the phrase to indicate that there are so many holes in his clothes that the wind blows in and out through them

6 **slave** person of the lowest class, but not a slave in the modern sense

7 **out of service** Wagner is using a pun to show both that Clown's clothing is 'out of service' (i.e. worn out) and that Clown himself is 'out of service' (i.e. unemployed)

9 **though it were** even if it was

11 **by'rlady** 'by Our Lady' – an oath, swearing by the Virgin Mary

13–14 **go like *qui mihi discipulus*** walk about dressed as my attendant (the Latin phrase means 'you who are my pupil'); Wagner is offering to supply Clown with clothes

16 **beaten silk** a costly fabric, but also a pun on 'beaten', as Wagner will feel free to hit his servant

stavesacre flea powder

17 **knavesacre** the land owned by a knave (a fool or a criminal), possibly the six feet of ground required to bury someone. Clown implies that Wagner's father was either a fool who left his son very little, or else a criminal who was executed. This was a common abusive joke at the time, and not very offensive

24 **presently** immediately

25 **familiars** agents of the Devil in the form of pet animals; witches were often thought to have a cat or a toad as a 'familiar'

30 **guilders** gold coins

31 **Gridirons** implements for spit-roasting meat also used by torturers and, by extension, presumed to be used in hell

33 **'Mass** oath, short for 'by the Mass'. All Clown's oaths suggest that he still follows Catholic forms, and so is very out of date in the strongly Protestant 1580s (see Historical Background)

44 **knock** hit

47 **tall** strong and tough

round slop loose trousers

s.d. **crying** shouting and yelling and generally creating a comic hullabaloo

53 **clefts** slits (a crude remark, concealed as a comment on cloven hooves)

63 **plackets** skirt fronts (pun: private parts)

69–70 **quasi vestigias nostras insistere** incorrect Latin meant to be translated as: 'as if to tread in our footsteps'

71 **Dutch fustian** literally, a kind of cloth; figuratively, meaningless speech

SCENE 5   Despite repeated hesitations, Faustus signs his soul over to the Devil. In exchange he receives information, textbooks, visitations by apparitions, and a visit from a devil dressed as a woman. Repeated appearances by the Good and Evil Angels are followed by Lucifer himself and a parade of the Seven Deadly Sins. The scene ends with Faustus still on the side of the Devil

The scene opens with Faustus in his study, pondering on the likelihood of damnation. The Good Angel and the Evil Angel make their first appearance and briefly plead with Faustus. They leave and Mephastophilis enters with the message from Lucifer that the bargain will go ahead, provided Faustus writes it in blood. Faustus questions Mephastophilis about the nature of hell. He then attempts to write with his blood but finds that at first it will not flow. A message appears on Faustus's arm, advising him to flee, but before he can think about its meaning, Mephastophilis distracts him with a group of dancing devils.

The signed deed of gift is handed over, and Faustus immediately begins to ask for the knowledge that he has been promised. He demands a wife, but Mephastophilis brings a lewd devil in the shape of a woman. Faustus next requests a book of magic spells, a book of astronomy, and one of botany. These appear, but are unsatisfactory and Faustus again thinks of heaven. The Good and Evil Angels immediately appear, speak three lines between them, and leave. Faustus returns to his earlier opinion that he cannot repent, and calls on Mephastophilis to discuss the nature of the world. Again, Mephastophilis's information strikes Faustus as limited and inaccurate. Furthermore, Mephastophilis is not permitted to conduct theological discussion. Faustus dismisses him in disgust, and the Good and Evil Angels return. At that moment, when Faustus seems to be in the middle of a repentance speech, the most powerful devils – Lucifer and Belzebub – appear with Mephastophilis. They threaten Faustus, and then display their power with a parade of the Seven Deadly Sins, each of whom describes his or her special characteristics. Faustus is impressed by this, and plans a visit to Hell.

This lengthy scene can be understood as a narrative sequence of four phases, which is repeated four times (with significant differences on the fourth repetition). Again and again, Faustus comes close to saving himself – but each time the powers of darkness bring on a yet more spectacular demonstration of their abilities, and Faustus finally falls further than ever from the possibility of repentance. The pattern of each phase is as follows:

- Faustus expresses doubts
- Persuasive efforts are made to influence him (either by the Angels or by supernatural shows)
- Faustus becomes more resolute
- Faustus enjoys the gains of his devilish contract.

The first (and briefest) cycle establishes this pattern:

- Doubt (lines 1–14): Faustus contemplates the apparent inevitability of damnation and the possibility of repentance
- Persuasion (lines 15–21): the Good and Evil Angels take turns to put their cases
- Resolve (lines 22–9): at midnight, Faustus calls up Mephastophilis (see Critical Approaches on Time)
- Gains (lines 30–60): the contract must be signed in blood; Mephastophilis satisfies Faustus's curiosity about the soul.

The pattern is then repeated:

- Doubt (lines 61–81): Faustus cuts his arm, but warning indications appear – the blood congeals unnaturally so he cannot sign, and words appear on his arm telling him to flee
- Persuasion (lines 82–7): Mephastophilis distracts Faustus with a show. Only occupying five lines in print, this persuasion could be lengthy on stage, as it includes a dance of devils
- Resolve (lines 88–113): Faustus stands by the written contract
- Gains (lines 114–74): Mephastophilis answers Faustus's questions, and brings him a whore (instead of the requested wife) and books.

The third cycle begins when Faustus recognises that the scientific information provided by Mephastophilis's books is inadequate:

- Doubt (lines 175–87): seeing the heavens reminds Faustus of God
- Persuasion (lines 188–93): the two Angels speak briefly

- Resolve (lines 194–208): Faustus considers the pleasures he has gained, and the extraordinary visions he has seen
- Gains (lines 209–40): Faustus and Mephastophilis discuss 'astrology' – the relationship of the stars and the planets from a scientific point of view.

From the discussion of astrology Faustus realises that Mephastophilis's knowledge is very limited, as is his power, and this brings Faustus to his most extreme moment of hesitation as he considers the wisdom of denying God. The fourth phase has significant differences – this time the processes of persuasion and resolve are repeated within the cycle:

- Doubt (lines 248–52): Faustus banishes Mephastophilis to hell
- Persuasion (lines 253–6): the Angels speak, and this time the Good Angel at last succeeds in being heard
- Resolve towards virtue (lines 257–8): Faustus calls on Christ to save his soul. This is a climactic moment in *Doctor Faustus*, which (despite its brevity) is perhaps equal in intensity to a major line in the closing scene of the play
- Repeated persuasion (lines 259–67): the most powerful devils, Lucifer and Belzebub, appear with Mephastophilis, and terrify Faustus into submission
- Resolve towards evil (lines 268–80): Faustus vows to think and speak only of devilish things
- Gains (lines 281–346): Faustus is rewarded with a pageant of the Seven Deadly Sins, each of which he cross-questions. Faustus's ultimate curiosity is to see hell and return, and the scene closes with the devil promising to deliver that hollow privilege. Faustus is thus committed to Mephastophilis again.

The effect of the repeated phases is to construct a tension in the audience, in which we continually hope that Faustus will repent, and are repeatedly disappointed. Nevertheless, the possibility that he might yet repent remains with us, for it gradually becomes clear that the sense of ultimate commitment to the Devil is an illusion – a misunderstanding on Faustus's part of the nature of God's mercy. As with a piece of music, the repetitions are not identical, but build in subtly different ways to the climax, in which Faustus calls on

God. Once that peak has been reached, however, the tension is pushed still higher by the appearance of Lucifer, and his fateful ability to manipulate Faustus's weakness. (See also Critical History & Broader Perspectives for Nicholas Brooke's alternative view that Faustus has genuine understanding of what he is trying to do.)

The scene focuses the major strands in the first part of the play: intellectual curiosity, Faustus's moral hesitations, and the spectacular displays put on by the Devil to keep him happy. The three strands are interwoven, as each one responds to the one before in a rhythmic manner which builds to an impressive stage climax in the **allegorical** parade of the Seven Deadly Sins. The Sins are more than just a display: they establish standards by which other characters can be judged. They **implicitly** also raise questions about Faustus's own sins: Pride and Envy, certainly, and also Lechery. The scene also develops our understanding of Mephastophilis as a character (see Characterisation).

The 'gains' that Faustus receives from his contract are remarkably worthless and empty. The visions he sees are, after all, neither real nor lasting, but temporary distractions. Instead of a wife, for example, he is offered a devil dressed up as a whore (since Mephastophilis cannot be involved with such Christian rites as marriage). As distractions, these shows are rather like a theatrical performance and in this sense *Doctor Faustus* may be offering the audience a **satirical** vision of themselves as resembling Faustus in their worldly pursuits.

The theatrical potential in the hugely entertaining shows put on for Faustus can be thought through imaginatively while reading this scene (see also Staging): the stage directions are brief, but in performance these would be much expanded by dances and action. Even the appearance of Lucifer and Belzebub needs to be carefully envisaged for maximum terror. In the parade of the Seven Deadly Sins, each has a speaking part, but one could also visualise various ways in which they might be costumed, ranging from the realistic through caricature to the grotesque. In modern productions, for example, they have appeared with huge carnival heads (Royal Shakespeare Company, 1970); as 'wispy, trailing' marionettes

(Royal Shakespeare Company, 1974, reviewed by Michael Billington); and with Lechery pushing Sloth in a pram (Royal Exchange Theatre, Manchester, 1981).

3 **What boots it?** what's the use?

23 **signory of Emden** governorship of the German city of Emden

29 ***Veni, veni Mephastophile*** (Latin) 'come, come Mephastophilis'

32 **So he will buy** provided that he will buy

42 ***Solamen miseris socios habuisse doloris*** (Latin) 'comfort of sorrows is to have companions in miseries'; or, 'misery loves company'

50 **bind** a pun playing on the meanings 'promise' and 'bandage'

54 **my proper blood** my own blood – a moot point, since it may be seen as belonging to God; Faustus appears to address the issue when he asks himself: 'Is not thy soul thine own?' (line 68)

64 **staying** stopping

s.d. **chafer** warming dish

74 ***Consummatum est*** (Latin) 'it is completed'; a blasphemous phrase, quoting the last words of Christ on the cross

77 ***Homo fuge*** (Latin) 'flee, man'

104 ***by these presents*** with this contract

122 **one self place** one identifiable place

147 **A plague on her** a curse: 'may she catch the plague!'

148 **toy** trivial thing

153 **Penelope** the patient, faithful wife of Odysseus in Greek mythology

154 **Saba** the Queen of Sheba

157 **iterating** speaking

163 **fain would I** I would very much like

188 **yet God will pity thee** God will still pity you

201 **despair** suicidal wishes (see Historical Background)

202 **blind Homer** the bardic author of the epic Greek poems the *Iliad* and the *Odyssey*; Homer was traditionally said to be blind

203 **Alexander's love, and Oenon's death** a tragic story from the *Iliad*

204 **he that built the walls of Thebes** the poet and bard Amphion, whose music had the power to make the walls build themselves according to Greek mythology

216 **axletree** axle – i.e. all planets move around the same axis

220–1 ***situ et tempore*** (Latin) 'place and time'

231 **freshmen** first-year undergraduate students

232 **dominion** one of the supposed classes of angels

232 *intelligentia* angelic spirit

240 *Per inaequalem motum respectu totius* (Latin) 'by an irregular movement in relation to the whole system'

244 **Move me not** don't try to persuade me

256 **rase** scrape

279 **mark** watch

285 **Ovid's flea** Roma Gill explains (p. 37): 'The poet of "Song of the Flea" ... envies the flea for its freedom of movement over his mistress' body.' Such a flea has already been mentioned by the clown in Scene 4

285 **corner** an obscene reference to the female genitalia

289 **cloth of arras** woven tapestry from the Flemish town of Arras

313 **bevers** drinks; refreshments

317 **Martlemas-Beef** salt beef

320 **March-Beer** strong beer

331–2 **an inch of raw mutton better than an ell of fried stockfish** an obscene and rather obscure phrase meaning, roughly, that Lechery prefers a man's penis to be short and powerful, rather than long and flaccid

332–3 **the first letter of my name** a common illogical joke. In this particular context, it is perhaps also playing on the fact that the letter 'L', pronounced 'ell', sounds like 'hell'

338 **O might I** I wish I could

343 **chary** carefully, dearly

SCENE 6   **Two ostlers make plans to use a magic book stolen from Faustus to gratify their appetites for drink and women**

Time has passed and Faustus has become famous. An ostler, Robin, has stolen one of his books of spells. Robin boasts to his friend Rafe of his plans to seduce a woman with its help. He also offers to get Rafe drunk for free, and to cast a spell to make the kitchen maid sexually willing. Rafe is delighted by this idea and so agrees to cooperate with devilish practices.

A relaxed scene between two servants shows how Faustus's behaviour is contaminating the morals of the lower orders of society. If we reverse the message, we can also see this scene as a comment on Faustus's magical achievements, showing them up as nothing more than gilded versions of the sordid and commonplace. Robin and Rafe both use language which mixes a pious consciousness with their corrupt desires, thus displaying unresolved incongruities, and perhaps inadvertently hinting that piety has the durability of custom. For example, Robin's maidens are from 'our parish' (line 4); and Rafe believes the parson's advice (line 26). Robin and Rafe will reappear in Scene 8.

2 **i'faith** an oath, short for 'in good faith' – i.e. 'I vow'

   search some circles make magical signs (pun: explore women sexually)

6 **tarries** waits

17 **his forehead** the location where a cuckold's horns are traditionally said to grow. When the Knight in Scene 9 is given a stag's horns on his head, the implication is that he is married to an unfaithful woman

17–18 **to bear with me** to conceive children by me

24 **'ipocrase** hippocras: a sweet mulled wine

28 **turn her and wind her** puns meaning both 'persuade her' and 'have sex with her'. Both phrases are jokes on Nan's role in the kitchens, turning the handle of the spit to roast meat

31 **horsebread** food for horses

CHORUS 2   Wagner explains that Faustus has gone to Rome

Wagner, alone on the stage, describes Faustus's progress in the art of conjuring, claiming that he has ridden in a chariot pulled by dragons to the top of Olympus, the mountain home of the Ancient Greek gods. Faustus's next project is to try out the efficacy of his learning at the Pope's court, where a feast is about to be held.

This Chorus, like the others, is directed at the audience. It functions to suggest a considerable passage of time between Scene 5 and Scene 7. The action about to unfold in Scene 7 is placed in the present tense with 'now' (line 7), and the audience is invited to believe that it is watching Faustus's story take place in the present. Wagner's language is dignified and glamorous, using **polysyllables** ('astronomy', 'firmament'), richly visualised images ('yoked dragons' necks') and elegant phrases ('as I guess') to suggest Faustus's enjoyment of the glories of his bargain. As his servant, Wagner participates in the adventures with delighted awe.

7 **to prove cosmography** to test his knowledge of the physical world (including the heavens and the earth)

SCENE 7   Faustus, invisible, disrupts a papal feast

In Rome, Faustus recounts his magical travels through European countries. Mephastophilis instructs Faustus in the layout of Rome, and makes him invisible. The Pope, the Cardinal of Lorraine and a parade of attendant friars enter for a feast. Each dish is snatched by Faustus, who concludes by boxing the Pope on the ear, and the prelates then exit. A group of friars return to chant a formal curse on Faustus. This triggers a frantic display of beatings and fireworks by the still-invisible Faustus.

This scene opens by giving us a sense of the exotic: of glamorous foreign travel achieved with ease. Humour follows, with the iconoclastic mockery of self-important figures – from the confusion and helpless anger of the Churchmen who cannot see their invisible tormentors to the bathos of the friars' formal cursing. This needs to be interpreted in the light of the Elizabethan attitude to Catholicism, which was banned, and to the Pope, who was widely reviled (see Historical Background for discussion of religion). As such, he was treated as a figure of fun or else as a threat, and even commonly referred to as the Antichrist (or Devil). There is thus an ironic joke here for Marlowe's audience that one set of 'devils' is tormenting another.

One may ask how to represent invisibility on stage, given that Faustus and Mephastophilis both have lines to speak and actions to perform. Lighting effects may help, or a cloak representing invisibility could be flung over Faustus, but it is usually sufficient for the victims simply 'not to see' them. The horseplay may seem childish when reading the bare text, but can be very effective on stage, especially if the Churchmen are made to look self-indulgent or worldly, or even to resemble eminent contemporary figures known to the audience – *Doctor Faustus* can in this way exploit the theatre's capacity to make contemporary political or social comment.

The scene could be played in different ways to convey different implications about Faustus. It could be a highly entertaining diversion, and carry us along with its flow of slapstick comedy, as suggested above. Alternatively, its childishness could be stressed, suggesting that the intellectual Faustus's pleasures have become debased and puerile. The Faustus we see here has become very dependent on Mephastophilis, who is subtly corrupting Faustus's finer feelings: instead of seeing the great sights of Rome as Faustus wishes, Mephastophilis suggests making fun of the Pope.

2 **Trier** German town situated on the Moselle river, founded by the Romans as the capital of Gaul

9 **Campania** the province around Naples, in Southern Italy

13 **Maro** the Ancient Roman poet Virgil, author of the epic *Aeneid*

16 **Venice, Padua, and the rest** Italian cities, and seats of Renaissance learning

31 **Tiber** the river that flows through Rome, as Mephastophilis correctly explains

35 **Ponte Angelo** a bridge over the Tiber built by Emperor Hadrian

43 **Styx, Acheron, and the fiery lake / Of ever-burning Phlegethon** the rivers of the Underworld in Greek mythology. Faustus swears by pre-Christian (hence pagan) aspects of death

48 **fain** gladly, willingly

51 **Whose *summum bonum* is in belly-cheer** who value eating and drinking above all other things. The Latin phrase *summum bonum*, meaning highest (or supreme) good, is usually applied to high pious or ethical ideals; to use it in relation to eating and drinking (i.e. gluttony, one of the Seven Deadly Sins) creates a **paradox** which indicates how far these priests have fallen away from their religious commitments

52 **to compass then some sport** therefore to devise and perform some entertainment

s.d. *sennet* trumpet call, fanfare

59 **fall to** begin (to eat)

s.d. *crosseth himself* makes the sign of the cross by touching first the left then the right shoulder, then the forehead, then the waist, in order to invoke the blessing of Christ and thus also protect against the Devil *s.d.* **a box of the ear** a sharp blow on the ear with a closed fist

80–1 **bell, book, and candle** instruments of the Catholic Mass

89 **Maledicat Dominus** (Latin) 'May the Lord curse him'

98 **Et omnes sancti** (Latin) 'and all the saints' – i.e. 'and may all the saints also curse him'

SCENE 8 **Robin and Rafe attempt to steal a goblet and are punished by Mephastophilis**

Still using the stolen book of magic from Scene 6, Robin and Rafe have stolen a silver goblet from a vintner. He searches them, but they use Faustus's book to make it invisible. In the process they incompetently, and probably accidentally, call up Mephastophilis, who terrifies them with fireworks. He resents having travelled all the way from Constantinople to answer their spell, and transforms them into an ape and a dog. They are capable of seeing the bright side of this, and plan to eat well in their new forms.

This scene continues the theme of eating and drinking (here in terms of the theft of food) which is also present at a higher social level in Scene 7, and which was begun by the character of Gluttony in Scene 5. In a curious reversal of expectations, this **low comic** scene shows Mephastophilis supporting the social *status quo* instead of subverting it: he makes it clear that servants must be kept in their place, and we see a demonstration of how frightening he can be if the magician's controlling skill is less than perfect. The transformation into animals could take place on stage, with the actors putting on large masks or animal heads, or it could (perhaps less effectively) be represented as a plan for the future.

Each of the characters seems more human to us after this scene (despite the change in physical form of Robin and Rafe). Mephastophilis shows himself liable to a natural irritability after a long journey, while Rafe and Robin could be seen as resilient and enterprising whether their circumstances are good or bad. To cope readily with the transformation into animals perceived as servile involves either great stupidity (as was probably originally intended) or great mental flexibility: readers should decide for themselves which interpretation they favour and why.

SCENE 8 continued

   2 **Ecce signum** (Latin) 'behold the evidence'

   6 **gull** trick, make a fool of

     Drawer barman

   8 **Soft sir** gently, sir (i.e. do not leave in a rush)

 12 **with your favour** with your permission

 14 **somewhat** something

     your fellow your friend (literally, 'the person just like you')

24–5 **Sanctobulorum Periphrasticon** (confused Latin and Greek) 'the thesaurus of the saints'

26–7 **Polypragmos Belseborams framanto pacostiphos tostis Mephastophilis, &c ...** (confused Latin and Greek, and some meaningless words) a name reminiscent of 'Belzebub' is jumbled with 'Mephastophilis' and words to do with meddling

 28 **O nomine Domine** (incorrect Latin) 'O name of the Lord'. This and the following two phrases sound like badly remembered phrases from the Latin church service

 30 **Peccatum peccatorum** (Latin) 'the sin of the sinners'

 31 **Misericordia pro nobis** (incorrect Latin) Robin jumbles the word for 'mercy' with a phrase meaning 'pray for us'

 47 **enow** enough

 49 **potage** a thick bean soup; one of the simplest foods eaten by ordinary people

CHORUS 3 **Faustus has returned home and greeted his friends, before meeting Emperor Charles V**

Sated by travel, Faustus has returned to Wittenberg, where he finds old friends who have missed him. They engage in their old entertainments of disputes and dialogues – Faustus's learning is spectacularly improved. Hearing of his skill, the Emperor Charles ('Carolus' in Latin) has invited him to visit, and we are told that he is now at the Emperor's court.

As with Chorus 2, this Chorus acts as a link between the dramatically rather disconnected episodes (Scene 7 and Scene 9) of Faustus's peripatetic life. It is possible that the author intended Wagner to perform this speech (since it is Wagner who speaks as Chorus 2 and Chorus 4), and the casting makes sense from the point of view of economy, though it is not specifically indicated in the original text. Indeed, one might consider the effects of using another character to give this speech: perhaps Mephastophilis, or even Pride? Either of these, by his or her presence alone, would point up the emptiness of Faustus's achievements. Using the Good Angel or the Old Man (in advance of his appearance in Scene 12) would give the impression of a sorrowing observer, watching Faustus's decline. The content of the speech indicates the warmth that Faustus's old friends feel for him, and his status as a wonder to the wider world.

1 **ta'en** taken

3 **stayed his course** stopped travelling

4 **such as bare his absence but with grief** those who only tolerated his absence with sorrow – i.e. those who missed him

6 **gratulate** welcome

11 **admired** expressed surprise

14 **Carolus the fifth** Charles V, Holy Roman Emperor, who held court at Innsbruck (see also Chronology)

16 **trial** display

SCENE 9   **Faustus gives the Emperor a magic show, by conjuring an appearance of devils precisely resembling Alexander the Great and his consort. He causes horns to appear on the head of a sceptical knight, before making plans to end his days in Wittenberg**

Emperor Charles V kindly (if misguidedly) promises Faustus that he can practise magic in safety. Faustus speaks humbly, addressing Charles as 'My gracious sovereign' (line 12), and is happy to perform the Emperor's self-aggrandising request to cause images of his ancestor Alexander the Great and Alexander's Queen to appear. These will be exact replicas, created by devils, rather than the real thing. A sceptical knight begins to irritate Faustus with his scornful remarks, and then leaves the stage. The conjuring takes place and even the Emperor believes the spectres to be genuine. When this display is over, Faustus asks the Emperor to send for the knight, who reappears, now decked with a pair of stag's horns, the humiliating symbol of sexual betrayal. Faustus claims that he had the horns put on to entertain the Emperor rather than out of vindictiveness towards the knight. After the departure of the Emperor and his court, the scene closes with Faustus confiding in Mephastophilis that his twenty-four years of power are nearly over and he will end his days in Wittenberg.

The contradictory moments in this relatively calm scene show how Faustus has used his skills and how different his life has been from the one he had planned. We see, for example, how out of character the bookish scholar's desire for world domination was, as expressed in Scene 1, and how unlikely it was that this gentle man could succeed in making himself into a tyrant. This scene contains no sign of Faustus's earlier hesitation or reluctance over his devilish contract. We might conclude that he is content with the way things have gone – but perhaps this calmness comes from Faustus's having ceased to recognise that his actions will have dreadful consequences.

Faustus has an excellent courtly manner, receiving graciously the Emperor's guarantee of immunity from punishment. The promise is erroneous if taken in the widest sense: the audience sees the **dramatic irony** that Faustus will eventually suffer damnation for his magic skill, and that this is quite out of the Emperor's hands. Again, the gentle Faustus is subservient to the Emperor, flattering him in ways that show that Faustus has no political power, and is as much caught up in hierarchies of respectfulness and etiquette as anyone. For all his skill, Faustus is not the social equivalent of the Emperor as he had planned to be – instead, this very class-conscious play shows him to be rather thrilled with invitations to the residences of the nobility of Europe.

Faustus has a scientist's honesty about detail, explaining carefully that the authentic body of Alexander has long since decayed and cannot be resurrected. Even in relation to embarrassing the critical knight, Faustus is keen to preserve some kind of reputation for virtue, in asserting (rather incredibly) that he was not being vindictive. This cannot easily be squared with his commitment to demonic forces, who presumably are not very concerned about being nice to people. Even his closing conversation with Mephastophilis has a chatty, domestic quality, as if between old friends. One effect of this construction of Faustus as a likeable character is to gain the audience's sympathy for him, thus intensifying the horrors of the damnation to come. In several ways, then, this scene can be seen as the calm before the storm, a structural break before the intensities that are to conclude the play.

5 **what thou list** whatever you want

13 **published** publicised (not necessarily in book form)

13–14 **nothing answerable** no match

14–15 **for that** because

18 **set** seated

28 **motion** mention

39 **so far forth as** as far as

42 **If it like your grace** I hope you don't mind (a polite expression)

45 **marry** (exclamation) goodness!

52 **Go to** begin

presently immediately

56 **Diana** goddess of the hunt in Roman mythology

57 **Actaeon** a mythical hunter who happened to see Diana while bathing. She turned him into a stag as a punishment and he was hunted and killed by his own hounds

59 **and you go to conjuring** if you are about to start conjuring

78 **no haste but good** a proverb, which Faustus seems to use to mean 'it is good to take things slowly'

94 **thread of vital life** Faustus is alluding to the Ancient Greek myth in which the Fates were said to spin a thread for each person's life, and cut it at an arbitrary moment

SCENE 10   **Faustus plays a series of tricks on a horse-trader**

Faustus has turned a bundle of hay into a fine-looking horse, which he passes off as genuine and sells, after a little bargaining, for forty dollars to a horse-courser. Faustus warns him not to ride the horse into water, and he leaves, after accidentally insulting Faustus by suggesting that he might function as a horse-doctor. Faustus briefly considers who he really is, then falls asleep.

Furious and soaking wet, the horse-courser returns to explain that when he rode the horse into a pond, it turned back into hay and dropped him in the water. Trying to force a refund of his money, the horse-courser attempts to wake the deeply sleeping Faustus by shouting and then by pulling on his leg. This falls off in the horse-courser's hand, but Mephastophilis allows him to escape on promise of a further forty dollars. Needless to say, the detachable leg was a trick, and Faustus will now be the richer by eighty dollars. At the end of the scene, Wagner appears with news of an invitation from the Duke of Vanholt.

> Towards the end of his life, Faustus is now himself involved in the **low comic** scenes, using his magic to gain trifling sums of money and to astonish the uneducated – scarcely feats that require supernatural power. For a moment (lines 24–9), he thinks more seriously about the afterlife, but finds comfort in the thought of Christ's forgiveness. His actions, however, contradict these thoughts, as he soon goes on to profit from crooked dealings which have much in common with the thefts attempted by Robin and Rafe in Scenes 6 and 8. The scene can thus be regarded as indicating Faustus's descent to the level of the servant class which he so much despises. For much of this scene he speaks in earthy **prose** (as do Robin and Rafe in the earlier scenes), rather than the more dignified **blank verse** which dominates his speech elsewhere.

> Alternatively, the scene can be interpreted as one in which Faustus chastises the greed of the horse-courser, just as he has chastised the pride and gluttony of the Pope in Scene 7. (These sins have already appeared in the pageant of the Seven Deadly Sins in Scene 5, alerting the audience to their presence in subsequent characters.) In that case, Faustus functions as a scourge of the wicked, even though he uses magic gained from the Devil to achieve it. This is coherent with his wishes to be seen as an honourable man, and may reveal how jumbled his own morality has become.

> The horse-courser assumes that Faustus can cure horses' illnesses, a confusion which angers Faustus, but which causes him to reflect on who and what he really is (lines 23–4):

>> Away, you villain! What, dost think I am a horse-doctor?
>> What art thou, Faustus, but a man condemned to die?

Verse is used, appropriately, when his mind turns to more serious matters. Faustus was once so clear in his mind, and – despite his hesitations about commitment – knew precisely who he wanted to be, what he wanted to do, and the price he was prepared to pay. He now seems to be losing that clarity and sense of identity, through years of playing with illusions of reality and trickery. Loss of social status for an Elizabethan was equivalent to a loss of personal identity. Faustus has been socially mobile and (as evident in Scene 9) clings ever more stubbornly to the *forms* of hierarchy, even while his actions create disorder in the physical world.

Faustus takes refuge in an unnaturally deep sleep (Mephastophilis claims 'he has not slept this eight nights'), from which he wakes to return to his behaviour as a petty charlatan, materialising a false leg for the horse-courser to tear off – a trick which is more shocking and repulsive than it is comic. In marked contrast, he reacts to the Duke of Vanholt's invitation in a spirit of urgent generosity which is close to servility.

  1 **Fustian** coarse cloth: the horse-courser gets Faustus's name wrong

  9 **a great charge** a heavy (financial) burden – Mephastophilis is being sarcastic

 12 **at any hand** in any circumstances

 17 **made man** a rich man

18–19 **hey ding ding, hey ding ding** Roma Gill (p. 55) suggests that 'The Horse-courser seems to be wishing that the horse were a stallion, not a gelding'

 22 **his water** his urine

 29 **quiet in conceit** contented with the idea

 30 **Doctor Lopus** Dr Lopez: a doctor at Queen Elizabeth's court (executed in 1594 for plotting to poison her); the name also sounds like Latin 'lupus', meaning both 'wolf' and a type of skin disease

 39 **bottle** a standard measurement of hay: a bundle, less than a bale

 41 **snipper-snapper** thieving servant

 42 **hey-pass** a conjuror's exclamation, similar to 'hey presto'

 58 **I am undone** I am in serious trouble

 64 **ostry** inn

 74 **I must be no niggard** I must give freely

SCENE 11   **Faustus impresses the Duke and Duchess of Vanholt by obtaining ripe grapes in the middle of winter**

The scene begins in the middle of Faustus's visit to the court of Vanholt (as is made clear by the Duke's first sentence in praise of entertainment already enjoyed). The Duchess is pregnant and expresses a craving for ripe grapes even though it is the middle of winter. Faustus provides her with a bunch of delicious grapes, explaining that they have come from the other side of the world where it is now summer. Gracious phrases are exchanged, Faustus is promised a reward, and all depart to continue the conversation elsewhere.

Here we see yet another display of Faustus's magical capacity and of his grasp of scientific explanation. Showing Faustus as a willing teacher distinguishes this scene from the **low comic** ones which precede it. He is represented as both a magician and a learned person. (We know now that the geographical details of his explanation are rather jumbled: the grapes would have come from the southern hemisphere, not the eastern.) Other recurrent themes appear here: Faustus's servility to the nobility, eating, and appetites which verge on the unnatural or gluttonous. Here too we see women treated as bodies rather than as people, a theme which reappears in relation to the image of Helen of Troy in Scene 12.

The scene is structured without an obvious narrative beginning or end. This technique of providing a 'snapshot' of a scene, with other events obviously taking place before and afterwards, is sometimes described as *in medias res* (Latin: 'into the middle of things'). It gives a powerful sense of the onward flow of events, and enhances the stage illusion of reality, with the audience positioned as casual bystanders, or even eavesdroppers on the action.

5 **great-bellied women** pregnant women
10 **meat** food in general
13 **so it would** if it would
21 **Saba** Sheba: the Middle East
28 **let us in** let's go indoors

CHORUS 4   Faustus approaches death with revelling

Wagner, on stage alone as the Chorus, reminds the audience of Faustus's approaching death. Now back in Wittenberg amongst his scholarly friends, Faustus is leading a drunken and self-indulgent life. It puzzles Wagner that Faustus continues to go to these wild student parties.

It seems that, in public at least, Faustus finds death of no concern, and his devil-may-care attitude can be seen as a **symbolic** assertion of his adherence to the demonic principles by which he has lived, and a rejection of Christian piety: drunkenness and gluttony have already been shown in the parade of the Seven Deadly Sins (Scene 5) to belong with the Devil.

It is arguable whether Faustus's bravado at this point in the play is sincere or hollow. Faustus may genuinely believe that he is safe from damnation, and simply involve himself in revelling out of *joie de vivre*. After all, he has said that he believes 'hell's a fable' (Scene 5, line 127) and Mephastophilis has told him that his ordinary life on earth counts as hell (Scene 5, lines 136–7). On the other hand, Faustus may be attempting the 'manly fortitude' that he has already recommended to Mephastophilis (Scene 3, line 86) as a way of successfully combating the fear of damnation. Finally, his earlier attempts to repent (for example, at Scene 5, line 187, and again at lines 257–8) may suggest that he is keeping this possibility in reserve for his last moments. The reader needs to decide which of these positions is the most persuasive, and why.

3 **if that death** if death
4 **carouse, and swill** get drunk in a rowdy way
8 **belike** probably

SCENE 12   Faustus conjures a vision of Helen of Troy. An Old
           Man advises him to repent, but Mephastophilis changes
           Faustus's mind, bribing him with Helen as a lover

Three scholars enter, having apparently been arguing over who was the most beautiful woman ever. Faustus conjures a vision of Helen of Troy, at the point in her life when she first arrived in Troy with Paris. Helen crosses the stage in complete silence. The scholars leave, filled with delight and praising both Helen's beauty and Faustus's achievement. Unexpectedly an Old Man enters, to point out to Faustus that his actions are in fact evil, and to persuade him to repent. Faustus reacts with **despair** and suicidal thoughts, which the Old Man forestalls.

During the Old Man's temporary absence, Mephastophilis threatens Faustus with torture if he reneges on his bargain, and Faustus yet again gives in, asking two favours. Viciously, he asks for devils to torture the pious Old Man; and in addition he asks to be able to possess Helen sexually.

The Old Man enters in time to observe Faustus kissing Helen and adoring her in lavishly poetic terms. Faustus and Helen depart, and devils enter to torment the Old Man. The scene closes on the latter's defiance of hell, and joyful welcoming of death.

> This scene follows directly from the Chorus, displaying what Wagner has just described, just as Scene 1 followed directly from the Prologue. Indeed, some editions of *Doctor Faustus* treat Chorus 4 and Scene 12 as a single scene (see Note on the Text).

> Narrative rhythm is important in this scene, and events are juxtaposed in such a way as to comment on one another. When the scholars depart they utter a rather incongruous blessing, 'Happy and blest be Faustus evermore' (line 24), which appears to call up the Old Man as if sent by God in response, in order to give Faustus yet another chance. After the **prosaic** simplicities of the **low comic** scenes, the language here has returned to the rich intensity of Scenes 3 and 5.

> Scene 12 re-uses the doubt–persuasion–resolve–gains pattern of events which structures Scene 5, but with a significant difference. The character of the Old Man takes on primarily the function of wise adviser, previously performed by the Good Angel, but also simultaneously the function of example, showing Faustus (and the audience) an ideal of behaviour in someone approaching death. The Old Man's words of persuasion paint vivid contrasting pictures of the joys of heaven and the pains of hell. Faustus's response is interesting, highlighting the difference between the patterns of Scene 5 and Scene 12. The persuasive moments in Scene 5 were in

the form of speeches – statements and arguments which were intended to change Faustus's mind – with Faustus simply following the last opinion expressed. Here, however, Faustus explains his ethical position; thus in being ethically comprehensible, Faustus's resolution in Scene 12 has a subtly different quality.

Faustus first suffers a fit of **despair**, but he also describes keeping his demonic bargain as 'to do thee right' (line 42), in other words, to be an honourable man. Logically, then, turning to God involves a betrayal of his purpose; while to betray God is, in a perverted kind of way, to be true to himself. Mephastophilis's image of the 'traitor' (line 57) picks up this anxiety, and it is this as much as the threat of being torn apart that persuades Faustus. It seems that he has now come to believe in hell, which he calls 'our hell' (line 68), contrary to Scene 5 where he asserts that 'I think hell's a fable' (line 127). Furthermore, both Faustus and the Old Man state quite clearly that faith in God keeps the soul safe and that extremes of physical suffering are irrelevant. If we take this point of view, we are forced to see Faustus as courageous in his dedication to hell. He boldly continues to use **paradox** with versatility when he takes the word 'sweet' from 'thy saviour sweet' (line 36), applies it to 'Sweet Mephastophilis' (line 60), and goes on to ask Lucifer (instead of God) for pardon.

In moving onward to show us Faustus enjoying his gains (as in the Scene 5 narrative pattern) this scene also gives the audience a doubled sense of illicit pleasure in the erotic spectacle of Faustus wooing Helen, and the sadistic spectacle of the Old Man's torture. Both episodes can be protracted on stage, to the limits of the director's wishes. At the same time, the audience can justify watching these scenes on the grounds that they have a pious message overall (see Literary Background on **Morality Plays**). The scene ends with the Old Man's triumphant cry of pleasure as he greets both death and God in poetry as memorable as Faustus's (lines 107–9):

> Ambitious fiends, see how the heavens smiles
> At your repulse, and laughs your state to scorn.
> Hence hell, for hence I fly unto my God.

This moment foreshadows Faustus's lines at the end of the play, greeting death and the Devil with horror.

3 **Helen of Greece** usually called Helen of Troy: Paris abducted Helen from her Greek husband Menelaus, thus beginning the ten-year-long Trojan War

13 **Sir Paris** an anachronistic title for Paris, making him seem like a medieval knight

14 **Dardania** Troy

s.d. ***passeth over*** walks across (in a slow and stately way)

19 **rape** abduction

24 **Happy** fortunate

26 **that I might prevail** I hope I can have an effect

36 **But mercy** except for mercy

59 **Revolt** turn again

66 **that base and crooked age** that lowly and bent Old Man

67 **durst** dares to

81 **the face that launched a thousand ships** Helen's beauty, which caused so many Greek ships to carry fighting men to Troy

82 **Ilium** Troy

84 **sucks forth my soul** Faustus imagines his soul passing out of his body in the kiss, but also realises that he is exchanging his soul for Helen's favours. As with the earlier apparition of 'Alexander and his paramour' (Scene 9), 'Helen' here is really a devil in human shape, but on this occasion Faustus has apparently forgotten that this is the case. 'She' may perhaps be a succubus – a kind of devil notorious for its predatory sexual behaviour

91 **thy colours** a scarf or other symbol of the person to whom a knight dedicated his efforts in battle
plumed crest helmet of a suit of armour, with feathers

92 **Achilles** a Greek warrior in the Trojan War, vulnerable only in his heel

97 **Semele** one of many women desired by Jupiter; she was burned by his divine glory

99 **Arethusa** a nymph in Ancient Greek mythology, desired by a river god, and so turned into a fountain

104 **sift me** torture me (to find out the virtuous parts)

108 **your state** the devils' impressive behaviour

SCENE 13   **Faustus explains the contract to the scholars. He passes his last night on earth alone, and goes to hell at midnight**

Frightened and regretful, Faustus greets his friends the scholars, explaining that he must shortly go to hell. He rejects their suggestions that he should repent, claiming that invisible devils hold his tongue and hands. The scholars withdraw to the next room to pray for him through the night. Faustus's long closing monologue concludes the scene, acting out the intense emotions of the last hour of his life in an anguished sequence of emotions and thoughts. These include: a desire for time to stand still; plans to call on God, frustrated by Lucifer's attacks; a fruitless desire to hide from divine anger and a list of places to hide; and a wish that he had not been born with a soul.

In a paroxysm of fear in the face of the doubled vision of God's rejection and Lucifer's ferocious welcome, Faustus is escorted to hell.

The hesitations about belief that have dominated the rest of the play are now completely cleared, and Faustus is well aware of the consequences of his contract. He no longer holds that 'hell's a fable' (Scene 5, line 127), or that only a comfortable pagan afterlife awaits him ('This word damnation terrifies not him, / For he confounds hell in Elysium' – Scene 3, lines 59–60). The pre-Christian thinkers whose words he earlier trusted are now seen as inaccurate: 'Ah, Pythagoras' *metempsychosis* – were that true, / This soul should fly from me' (Scene 13, lines 99–100). Extraordinarily, he is still divided over whether to repent or to follow Lucifer.

Paradoxically, although earlier in the play damnation was considered to be only a state of mind, Faustus here needs to be able to control his body in order to utter words of repentance, or to place his hands in prayer. The devils have complete control of his physical world, and hold him back from doing these things (see Themes regarding the body/soul duality). Comments from Faustus sprinkled through the scene reveal that the devils are already holding, pulling, pinching and tearing at him even before the time is up, for example lines 31–2: 'O, he stays my tongue! I would lift up my hands, but see, they hold them, they hold them!' The devil prevents him speaking a prayer, and several others hold his hands from assuming a praying position. At line 71, Faustus seems confused: 'O I'll leap up to my God! Who pulls me down?' He is not sure which devil, if any, is holding him back, and the possibility arises that much of this conflict takes place in his own mind. In lines 74–5 Faustus addresses the devils, then Christ, then Lucifer again:

> Ah, rend not my heart for naming of my Christ;
> Yet will I call on him – O spare me, Lucifer!

He feels a devil tearing at his heart because he has spoken the name of Christ. He insists on continuing the attempt to repent but is prevented by Lucifer's attacks and turns instead to pleading with Lucifer to stop, thus losing his last opportunity.

Throughout the speech, Faustus expresses the idea that his fate was inevitable from the moment of his birth – or even before. He begins to believe that it is a part of what he is, and he could only have avoided it by being born without a soul, or perhaps by having different parents. Faustus the free thinker now expresses the views of a fatalist. Even at line 106, where Faustus momentarily takes on partial responsibility for his decisions ('curse thy self'), he quickly slips into 'curse Lucifer', apparently blaming the Devil for his damnation. Even now, he does not understand the importance of the Old Man's example from Scene 12: that he is personally responsible for his own salvation. If, as some critics argue, Faustus was taking precisely that kind of personal responsibility for himself as an individual when he chose damnation (i.e. he was not choosing out of ignorance but making a responsible decision), this scene shows him weakening from being 'resolute' (Scene 1, line 133).

Faustus is almost insane in his desperation, and appears to believe that he can hide from God in the earth (lines 81–2) or in a mist (lines 85–6). Neither of these is feasible. He turns to further elements, namely air and water, in order to hide from the devils: 'Now body, turn to air' (line 108); 'O soul, be changed into little water drops' (line 110). Faustus is in a despicable, cowardly panic when he and his ambitions vanish to hell; his last word is 'Mephastophilis' – naming his old confederate in a tone which might be read as revulsion, terror, appeal, or all three together.

3 **chamber-fellow** room-mate

7 **Belike** probably

31 **stays my tongue** holds my tongue still

39 **a bill** a contract

52 **what noise soever** whatever noise

64 **Fair Nature's eye** the sun

68 ***O lente, lente currite noctis equi!*** (Latin) 'O run slowly, slowly, you horses of night!' Faustus is perhaps inappropriately expressing his desire for time to stand still in his choice of quotation: taken from Ovid's *Amores*, the words express the poet's wish for a longer night with his beloved

83 **stars that reigned at my nativity** the astrological position when he was born: his star-sign

89 **So that my soul may but ascend to heaven** if only my soul could rise to heaven

99 **Pythagoras'** *metempsychosis* Pythagoras was an Ancient Greek philosopher and mathematician, who was said to have believed that after death the soul could move from one body to another, whether human or animal

103 **elements** earth, water, air and fire: the medieval **elements**

E PILOGUE   **The Chorus laments Faustus's wasted possibilities**

With calm and dignity the Chorus sums up Faustus's tragedy as a lost opportunity for great virtue and learning. The Chorus invites the audience to learn from Faustus's example, and not to attempt any similar transgressions against divine law.

Likening Faustus to the branch of a tree, the Chorus sees him as ruined through being 'cut' and 'burned' – words which still carry the violence which closed the previous scene. Faustus, like the tree, might have grown well and fulfilled his best nature as a human being, had he not been 'cut', a technique which can be used to make trees grow crookedly or sideways. The image of the 'laurel bough' reminds us of his great achievements as a scholar even before he took to necromancy.

The Chorus stresses that our role is merely to observe these hellish doings, and not to attempt to copy them, thus picking up a theme of 'looking' in proper and improper ways, which has appeared elsewhere in the play. Generally, Faustus has looked at displays and books in mistaken or distracted ways, which have furthered his downfall. The audience, now, is asked to cope better than Faustus did: to observe this whole entertainment provided by the play of *Doctor Faustus*, and to be morally improved by it.

The short speech could be seen as an **elegy** for Faustus: the nearest he will get to a funeral speech. The tone is one of detachment and almost of smug superiority, which rather suggests that it should not be spoken by Wagner, or even by the scholar friends, all of whom seem to feel warmly towards Faustus. Its quality is more abstract, like a much later observer giving a historical judgement; a director might consider giving the speech to one of the more abstract virtuous characters, such as the Old Man or the Good Angel. The Chorus's use of old-fashioned **alliteration** ('fiendful fortune') and the neat final **couplet** provide a sense of **closure**.

2 **Apollo's laurel bough** in Greek mythology Apollo was the god of music and poetry. His emblem, the laurel, was traditionally awarded to the greatest poets

Terminat hora diem, terminat author opus (Latin) 'the hour ends the day, the author ends the work'

PART THREE

CRITICAL APPROACHES

CHARACTERISATION

Characterisation is often discussed in terms of 'rounded' characters (i.e. realistic and detailed) and 'flat' characters (i.e. simple and undeveloped). There are two main handicaps to seeing the characters in *Doctor Faustus* as rounded, namely **allegory** and brevity.

Doctor Faustus contains allegorical characters (some of them even lacking proper names) who represent abstract ideas such as Virtue (the Good Angel, the Old Man) and Evil (the Evil Angel, the Seven Deadly Sins). The Clown is an allegory of the concept of Ignorance, and even the devils Lucifer and Mephastophilis can be seen as allegories of the temptation to deny God. Allegorical figures can tend to be so single-minded that they are flat as characters.

The second handicap to full characterisation is the brevity of many of the minor characters' appearances on stage. This is a play with a large number of very short parts: only Faustus and Mephastophilis spend a significant amount of time on stage, or have lengthy speeches (Faustus himself is a more rounded character, as the play shows his reactions to a relatively wide variety of situations). The proliferation of minor characters gives an impression of the crowded world that Faustus inhabits, and of the wide-ranging nature of his contacts and experiences: the play cannot effectively show Faustus on his travels through the world, but it can instead show a multitude of encounters with people.

In spite of these points, sufficient material can be found by a careful reading of minor characters' speeches to produce richness and roundedness in performance. The writing of Marlowe (and his comic collaborator) is complex, and even a short passage conveys a variety of impressions economically: every word can be made to count. A play is, of course, designed to be performed, and thus the completed form of each character requires a real person to act the part, bringing to it all the quirks of personal appearances, mannerisms and tones of voice that the actor already possesses. These must be coherent with the part as written, but they also (literally) flesh it out. Therefore a play text needs to be read with the added consciousness of the possibilities it provides for performance. Considering each character separately allows readers to ask themselves what they can make of each word, and what it might imply about the character's personality, tastes, values and emotions.

Thus in the case of *Doctor Faustus*, the allegorical function does not necessarily prevent us from seeing these characters as rounded. Brevity is potentially a greater handicap, but even this is not necessarily problematic. After all, one of the most significant characters in the play is Helen of Troy, who has no lines at all, and very little time on stage.

The characters are discussed in the order in which they first appear on stage; beside each is a list of the scenes in which the character appears – this helps to identify which characters are never on stage simultaneously and so can be doubled in performance.

CHORUS (PROLOGUE, CHORUS 3, EPILOGUE)

The Chorus is a function rather than a true character, and operates as a neutral observer rather than a judge of Faustus's actions. The Chorus introduces and closes the play, and explains the passage of time between scenes. In some productions the part is doubled by the actor playing Wagner, since Choruses 2 and 4 are explicitly assigned to Wagner, but the **diction** of the Chorus is considerably more refined and **metaphoric** than Wagner's style elsewhere in the play. Experimentally, one might think of using a female actor in the role, which could give a greater sense of ironic detachment from the very masculine concerns of the Wittenberg scholars, and place a question against the Prologue's opening address to '(Gentlemen)'. Originally this role, like all others on the commercial stage at the time, would have been played by a man.

FAUSTUS (SCENES 1, 3, 5, 7, 9, 10, 11, 12 & 13)

Faustus is dominated by two main character traits: intellect and ambition. It is the intellect that creates doubt when ambition alone would simply carry him forward in his devilish contract, but it is also intellect that makes his ambition possible in the first place. Within these two, evidence can be found for a series of binary oppositions: he is capable of stupidity and intelligence; courage and cowardice; cruelty and generosity. In short, Faustus is filled with contradiction and so comes across as very human, especially in his ambition to better himself. To this extent Faustus is a **mankind figure**: a representative of each one of us. Faustus also tries to transcend that status, however, and this ambition to be greater than human is his downfall.

Fundamental to a production of the play is deciding who Faustus is – how to find the person within the folly, the pretentiousness and the intellect? Faustus feels intensely and expresses his feelings in richly evocative poetic language. He also values scholarship (in spite of his dismissive monologue in Scene 1), following his punishment of the knight in Scene 9 with the words 'hereafter speak well of scholars' (line 87). We need to see him as passionate, even though he believes himself to be logical: he is easily swept away by glamorous language and easily distracted by the devils' shows, which they put on each time he is about to reason his way through to the point of realising the need to repent. He has trouble telling the difference between reality and the imagination. In an **ironic** move, the play redefines practicality when it shows that Faustus's knowledge, which is about the real world, is actually impractical in comparison with an imaginative knowledge about virtue and godliness. Magic purports to draw the imagination and reality together (and so make it unnecessary for the practitioner to detect any difference between them).

Faustus's behaviour reveals a tension between solitariness and gregariousness. He is most comfortable when thinking aloud on his own in the great **soliloquies** (Scene 1, lines 1–63 and 78–99, for example) and he craves independence in his magic-making. The scholars remind us, however, that his earliest intellectual feats took place in a community with a tradition of public, spoken dialogue: 'Faustus, that was wont to make our schools ring with *sic probo*' (Scene 2, lines 1–2). Oddly, Faustus's greatest pleasures are taken when he is away from his friends, so that physical luxury is associated with the Devil and solitude from the human race, while rationality and asceticism seem to go with a sense of his equals' community.

Of humble origins himself, Faustus is immensely conscious of social class – though probably no more so than most people of Marlowe's period. Nevertheless, his habit of respect for nobility and disrespect for servants directly contradicts any Christian sense of human beings as equals – his little trick with the out-of-season grapes is no greater for having provided them to a Duchess.

WAGNER (SCENES 1, 2 & 4, CHORUSES 2 & 4)

Faustus's servant has a typically German name, signifying his ordinariness, not unlike calling an English character 'Johnson'. In the **Morality Plays** (see Literary Background), comic scenes depended on the antics of a group of lower-class characters whose main interests in life were eating, drinking and making rude jokes. Wagner inherits some aspects of this role: as a servant, he has a comic function in the play. He is pragmatic, but also adventurous in his willingness to undertake novel tasks, not just through loyalty to Faustus but also through a kind of intellectual curiosity. He images those simple folk who are led to believe that Faustus has achieved something great – who, in modern terms, would be the gullible consumers of media hype. He also emulates Faustus, showing that a great man can have a bad influence on those around him. The play is not concerned with Wagner's fate, though presumably his soul is as much in question as Faustus's.

Wagner is socially intermediate: though a servant, he is also capable on occasion of dignified, rational speech, especially when he speaks as the Chorus. This dignified, observing aspect of the role would be enhanced if he also delivered the speeches of the Prologue, Chorus 3 and the Epilogue, as many editions suggest he should.

The ways in which the Wagner character comments on Faustus's behaviour are therefore varied: he reflects Faustus in exaggerated form, showing how foolish Faustus is; he admires Faustus's achievements, showing how corrupting Faustus's irresponsible behaviour can be for others as well as himself; and he narrates events as an observer whose position changes during the course of the play from admiration to puzzlement.

GOOD ANGEL AND EVIL ANGEL (SCENES 1 & 5)

These always appear together as a matched pair and function as binary opposites. Most critics speak as if the characters are male, but technically angels have no sex. They could therefore be cast as men, women, or one of each, or perhaps as androgynous. The choices make a considerable difference. A production might profit from obvious gender stereotypes by casting the Evil Angel as a thuggish male, and the Good Angel as an innocent-looking blonde woman. Reversing this, to cast a sinful woman as the Evil Angel could bring out similarities between that character, the 'hot whore' (Scene 5) and Helen of Troy (Scene 12), and reinforce a misogynistic trend in the play. Androgynous or similarly dressed and presented characters will reject these gendered readings and stress the Angels' parallel dramatic functions as equal but opposite contenders for Faustus's beliefs.

The Good Angel focuses on the anger of God, to motivate Faustus to repent and cease practising black magic, and so foreshadows the angry God Faustus sees in Scene 13: 'My God, my God, look not so fierce on me!' (line 112). George Santayana noticed that 'the good angel, in the dialogue, seems to have so much the worst of the argument. All he has to offer is sour admonition and external warnings' (*Three Philosophical Poets*, Harvard University Press, 1910, pp. 147–9). The Evil Angel offers all the pleasures of the flesh in graphic terms, and goes on to contradict the Good Angel's assertion that Faustus can still be forgiven. On each occasion Faustus believes the angel who speaks last, and does not detect the Evil Angel's lies. On stage, of course, their 'names' are not public, and if there is no distinction in costume, Faustus and the audience cannot immediately detect which one must be the liar, as readers who have the benefit of speech headings can.

VALDES (SCENE 1)

Referred to several times as 'German Valdes', this character is one of the two magicians who lend Faustus their books and teach him the art of conjuring. He helps to persuade Faustus that magic will bring him the desired wealth and renown – one cannot help wondering, however, why Valdes and Cornelius are not themselves famous and wealthy, given their claims about magic. It may be that they are little more than devilish tempters themselves. Certainly they are not very competent magicians, since they believe in the power of their book, which is clearly not essential for bringing the devil to Faustus, as Mephastophilis points out in Scene 3, and is fairly useless in the hands of Rafe and Robin in Scene 8. It is

Valdes who suggests that beautiful women might be obtained by necromantic means (Scene 1, lines 127–9), thus initiating a theme which will run through the play.

CORNELIUS (SCENE 1)

The second tutor in magicianship encourages Faustus by suggesting that his knowledge makes him flatteringly appropriate for the magic arts: 'Faustus, these books, thy wit, and our experience / Shall make all nations to canonize us' (Scene 1, lines 119–20). It is Cornelius, too, who is keen for Faustus to try out his knowledge alone, making him more vulnerable to Mephastophilis: 'And then, all other ceremonies learned, / Faustus may try his cunning by himself' (Scene 1, lines 159–60). Together Valdes and Cornelius function as tempters of Faustus, describing to him the joys he might obtain, thereby taking a version of the role of the **vice-crew** from the **Morality Plays**. They do not reappear, perhaps for the practical reason that the actors may be needed to double other roles in the succeeding scenes, but their absence also gives a sense of Faustus's growing isolation from human company.

THE SCHOLARS (SCENES 2, 12 & 13)

Collectively, the Wittenberg scholars' main characteristic is loyalty and simple virtue. They are largely indistinguishable from one another, except that one is always more inclined to believe in the power of prayer than the others. They are intellectuals who enjoy Faustus's mental gymnastics and are impressed by his learning as much as his magic. They do, however, cause him to call up Helen of Troy, who Faustus finds ultimately desirable. Their function in the plot is to assist the symmetry with which the ending answers the beginning: when Faustus eventually returns to Wittenberg, they are still there for him.

MEPHASTOPHILIS (SCENES 3, 5, 7, 8, 9, 10, 11, 12 & 13)

This is the second largest part, with Mephastophilis on stage during much of the play. Mephastophilis is a terrifying devil and a tempter, and so in a sense an enemy of Faustus. At one point he offers Faustus a dagger

(Scene 12) to encourage him to suicide and so damn himself, a quick way of ensuring the result that apparently still hangs in doubt at this late stage of the play.

Mephastophilis also inspires a certain sympathy. He is the victim of a single mistake, loyalty to Lucifer, and we can almost feel him on occasion attempting to warn Faustus not to commit the same error (Scene 3, lines 78–81):

> Think'st thou that I, who saw the face of God,
>
> And tasted the eternal joys of heaven,
>
> Am not tormented with ten thousand hells
>
> In being deprived of everlasting bliss!

At the same time as doing Lucifer's bidding, he also must honour the contract with Faustus to tell him the truth, and so comes across as strikingly honest. There is poignancy in his situation when he explains that he is one of the 'Unhappy spirits that fell with Lucifer, / Conspired against our God with Lucifer, / And are for ever damned with Lucifer' (Scene 3, lines 71–3). When Faustus enquires as to whether Mephastophilis suffers any pain, he answers: 'As great as have the human souls of men' (Scene 5, line 44). It is through Mephastophilis's perceptions of the nature of damnation, and of the beauty of what it means to have a human soul, that we see just what Faustus is throwing away: 'Think'st thou that heaven is such a glorious thing? / I tell thee 'tis not half so fair as thou, / Or any man that breathes on earth' (Scene 5, lines 181–3). Mephastophilis is an intellectual match for Faustus, comprehending the abstract proposition that hell is not so much a place as a state of mind – the condition of deprivation of God: 'Hell hath no limits, nor is circumscribed / In one self place; for where we are is hell, / And where hell is, must we ever be' (Scene 5, lines 121–3). In some productions he manifestly despises Faustus's folly in disbelieving him. In others he appears as a companion/servant, taking the place in Faustus's life of the Scholars and Wagner.

CLOWN (SCENE 4)

The Clown, a country bumpkin or yokel, is cheeky and clever but also lewd and uneducated. He represents common humanity from the world outside the courts and universities. He is cowardly when faced with the devils Baliol and Belcher, but also willing to earn an immoral living despite his residual Catholicism. He is thus a bundle of contradictions, and this irrationality is part of the humour of Scene 4.

BALIOL AND BELCHER (SCENE 4)

These are a male and a female devil, possibly naked, as Clown is able to make an obscene comment about them (Scene 4, lines 51–3). Non-speaking parts, they are energetic and violent: the roles could be performed with gymnastic skill, or perhaps as modern thugs. Whatever the final choice, they must be mobile and frightening.

LUCIFER AND BELZEBUB (SCENES 5 & 13)

These major devils are terrifying stage presences, whose fearful appearance is the kind of effect that one would be willing to pay extra to see. (In the **Morality Plays** of earlier in the sixteenth century, money was actually collected from the audience before the main devil would deign to appear. This does not happen in *Doctor Faustus*, but it is a helpful way of imagining how impressive the devils are supposed to be.) They may be performed in extraordinary ways, for example by puppets or stilt-walkers.

THE SEVEN DEADLY SINS (SCENE 5)

These fully **allegorised** figures – Pride, Covetousness, Wrath, Envy, Gluttony, Sloth and Lechery – each has a brief speech in character. They may be extravagantly and grotesquely costumed in stylised or **symbolic** ways.

ROBIN (SCENES 6 & 8)

This servant character is an enterprising stable-boy (ostler) and thief. He is ambitious to practise magic and corrupts his friend Rafe with temptation.

RAFE (SCENES 6 & 8)

The second stable-boy is not as clever as Robin, and has more moral objections, though these are easily overruled. He is tempted by the promise of sexual experiences. Like Clown, Robin and Rafe represent common humanity, but they also mirror Faustus's ambition, his persuadability and his approach to women. Seeing these traits as obviously foolish in these **low comedy** scenes helps the audience to perceive Faustus's parallel foolishness.

THE POPE AND THE CARDINAL OF LORRAINE (SCENE 7)

Although mainly serving as a butt for Faustus's abusive tricks, these two characters also represent the physical self-indulgence of Churchmen: the Pope is very persistent in his repeated attempts to eat and drink. To some extent, Faustus's attack on them would have been seen at the time as a reasonable scourging of a priesthood grown lax, and a sixteenth-century Protestant audience would have found the humiliation of the head of the Catholic Church side-splittingly funny (see Historical Background). The latter aspect would be particularly difficult to present on the modern stage.

FRIARS (SCENE 7)

These Churchmen are obedient to the Pope's orders, and set about their business with 'good devotion', even though the curse they chant contains preposterously trivial words, sung in an impressively solemn ritual manner.

VINTNER (SCENE 8)

We know very little about the character of the Vintner, except that he appears to be an honest working man, keen to defend his rights.

EMPEROR (SCENE 9)

Holy Roman Emperor Charles V is a representative of the aristocracy, gracious but not very bright. (Charles V was the father of Philip II of

Spain, whose Armada was defeated in 1588, around the probable date of composition of *Doctor Faustus*; see also Chronology.) He is self-important, even filled with pride (one of the Seven Deadly Sins) about his ancestry. If Faustus's magic serves to swell the Emperor's pride, and so to spread a tiny grain more of corruption in the world, then his magical display of apparitions cannot be regarded as innocent, but is instead the Devil's work.

KNIGHT (SCENE 9)

The knight at Charles V's court is turned into a laughing stock by Faustus, but not before he has shown great insight into the emptiness of the magician's art, and considerable courage in voicing his objections publicly.

HORSE-COURSER (SCENE 10)

Literally and metaphorically out of his depth, the brash and pushy horse-trader seeks to drive an advantageous bargain. He believes himself to be more articulate than he really is, getting names wrong and asking inappropriate questions. His sinister tendencies to mistrust and violence are punished in turn by near-drowning and then the shock of pulling Faustus's (false) leg off.

DUKE AND DUCHESS OF VANHOLT (SCENE 11)

Two further graciously aristocratic characters. One might consider whether the pregnant Duchess's craving for grapes is justified by her physical condition, or whether she is perhaps intended to be an example of female gluttony. The grapes are clearly real, not illusory magic, and she displays intellectual curiosity in asking Faustus how he obtained them.

OLD MAN (SCENE 12)

This elderly, virtuous and pious figure could be presented as slightly miraculous, since he appears just when Faustus needs blessing and holy advice most. His age can be seen as serving two purposes: first, the Old Man represents an image of Faustus himself, who by this point in the play (after twenty-four years have elapsed) is now also old; second, the Old Man is also a *memento mori* – a traditional medieval Christian reminder of the inevitability of death, and so of the need for repentance.

He feels intensely, and possesses the rhetorical abilities of a hellfire preacher to contrast the sweetness of heaven with an elaborately disgusting view of hell. He reasons well, explaining economically and precisely what Faustus must do in order to reach heaven. The Old Man's immense strength of character in the face of physical torture is due to his absolute, unshakeable faith in God, and he could perhaps be represented as extremely frail. He exemplifies what Faustus could have been, but manifestly is not.

HELEN (SCENE 12)

This apparition serves a key purpose, even though she says nothing. As absolute physicality she is the means by which Faustus finally, irrevocably dooms himself. She is a figure onto which Faustus projects his own idea of female perfection, in relation to which he can tolerate the idea of himself as a body without a soul. On stage, therefore, Helen should not necessarily appear as an Ancient Greek, but perhaps as a contemporary ideal: the kind of woman perceived as beautiful by the culture within which Faustus lives. She might, for example, replicate a picture on the wall of Faustus's study.

STRUCTURE

To some extent the apparent structure of *Doctor Faustus* in thirteen discrete scenes has been artificially imposed on it by editors. Some believe that five act divisions can be detected, thus many editions are divided into acts and scenes (see Note on the Text for further details). This kind of formal structure is helpful for identifying portions of text, but there are also overarching narrative patterns in *Doctor Faustus*:

- the **tragic** downfall of a great man: the loss of the possibility of greatness through a tragic flaw, in this case Pride
- the **Morality Play** structure (see Literary Background) of the gradual education of the spiritually naïve person to a recognition of the

nature of God, through a repeated sequence of blunders and moral
lessons

- a three-part structure in which the first part involves the serious
business of Faustus's seeking out the Devil and striking a bargain with
him; the middle part involves trivial entertainment and pastimes; and
the third section offers an intense poetic conclusion, balancing the
seriousness of the opening.

None of these structures is a perfect description of what takes place in
Doctor Faustus, but a combination of the three allows some useful
observations to be made.

The larger structure is composed of a set of self-contained scenes,
where at first sight only those at the beginning and the end seem to be
absolutely necessary for the plot, which is typically perceived as the bare
bones of the play's events. Many of these inner **episodic** scenes contain
characters who do not reappear, or only trivially where they do. On a
practical level, this allows for doubling of parts in performance, but on a
thematic level it creates a sense of a wide world, full of chance encounters,
and of a wide social spectrum of people, all of whom know Faustus. The
multiplicity of comic scenes thus effectively sketches the extent of
Faustus's fame, suggesting that everyone is involved, from the highest to
the lowest.

The comic scenes also have a crucial function as a kind of loose sub-
plot, commenting on events in the main plot by repeating them in a
slightly different form, and showing up the triviality of Faustus's
behaviour and achievements. Their language and choice of vocabulary
echo **satirically** the thematic concerns of the Faustian plot. Simple
colloquial speech becomes heightened in significance and thus
metaphoric, when placed in the context of the devilish contract of the
surrounding scenes. An example is the horse-courser's casual way of
saying hello and goodbye in Scene 10: 'God save you, master doctor' (line
2) and 'God b'y sir' (line 20) take on a special emphasis (the latter, spelt
'goodbye' in modern English, being a contraction of 'God be with ye').
Perhaps it is no coincidence that Faustus falls into a reverie on the subject
of death in the middle of this scene (see also Textual Analysis, Text 2).
These comic scenes are thus not at all dispensable, but can in fact be
understood as an essential part of the play.

The passage of time is handled with considerable skill in *Doctor Faustus*, moving at different speeds within the narrative of the play. The brisk biography of the Prologue summarises Faustus's early years in a few short sentences, and propels the play into the continuous present tense of natural time: 'And this the man that in his study sits' (Prologue, line 28). Thus the play's time and natural time initially run side by side. Subtly, however, Faustus's time accelerates: by the end of Scene 1 he decides to go to dinner, and during the few minutes of Scene 2 (in which the scholars worry about him) he has finished his meal and learned all there is to know about magic, ready to conjure at midnight at the beginning of Scene 4. This acceleration continues, documented by the comments and summary speeches of the Chorus, until twenty-four years of stage time have passed in around two hours or less of natural time.

Both the opening and closing monologues display this acceleration effect particularly clearly. As Faustus reaches the last evening of his life in Scene 13, a clock is heard striking eleven, and he begins to consider the passage of time: 'Ah Faustus, / Now hast thou but one bare hour to live' (lines 59–60); 'The stars move still, time runs, the clock will strike, / The devil will come, and Faustus must be damned' (lines 69–70). His monologue explicitly measures out half an hour – which takes thirty lines. The second half hour passes more quickly, taking only seventeen lines of monologue. Faustus talks obsessively about the passage of time, in his desperate, urgent need to hold it back – but it passes faster and faster. With this insight, we can now see that a similar process takes place in the opening monologue (Scene 1, lines 1–63), where Faustus rushes and pauses repeatedly with fatal inevitability through a review of the learning he intends to reject, towards the act which will initiate the whole process of his damnation.

Time in *Doctor Faustus* also takes several forms: a human lifetime; a circular structure of seemingly endless repetitions by which Faustus fails to learn; eternity; the duration of the play. The difference between human time and eternity is one that Faustus tries to control at the end of the play. He has failed to notice that his contract has already made time control Faustus himself: in naming the arbitrary duration of his power over Mephastophilis as twenty-four years, Faustus has submitted to time. Beyond this, time is godly – devils cannot control it, a fact which has been hinted at when Mephastophilis had to fetch the Duchess her ripe grapes by travelling at great speed to the other side of the world.

NARRATIVE TECHNIQUE

The narrative in *Doctor Faustus* involves an alternation between 'telling' and 'showing', begun by the Prologue's summary of Faustus's early life, which proceeds to hint strongly at what will follow in the scenes the audience is about to see. This habit of foreshadowing events was a popular one in Elizabethan stagecraft, and many plays include a **dumb show** which narrates the plot before it actually happens. In *Doctor Faustus*, the telling belongs largely to the Chorus, and is principally used to carry the scene through time or space: to fill in some knowledge of events that cannot credibly be shown on stage (such as a European tour, or a chariot pulled by dragons). The Chorus also copes with the passage of time, as it offers the audience an objective moment outside the events of the plot, when the action is suspended.

An intermediate kind of telling takes place when Faustus embarks on his monologues, detailing the thoughts and emotional events which he experiences. With this multiplicity of plots repeated in sub-plots, of telling followed by showing, and of Faustus's repeated enunciations of anxiety, comes the effect of multi-layered meanings, which is a speciality of this play. These inexorable variations on a theme bring both Faustus and the audience/reader closer and closer to the **dénouement**, building up tension and making the dénouement feel more and more important the longer it is delayed.

Much of the subtlety of the narrative is contained within the **ironic** and **paradoxical** language with which a tension is unremittingly sustained between what is said and what is believed. Faustus's belief structures are always in question, and generally shifting: the clues by which they can be traced are in the vocabulary he uses. Extra possibilities of meaning appear when Faustus refuses to resolve such contradictions, but seems to try to hold two opinions at once. Indeed, he finds the reallocation of pious terminology especially entertaining, and also a useful weapon. The apparently casual use of the word 'sweet' is a case in point. 'Sweet' is a prominent Christian epithet, and its force is demonstrated by the Good

Angel ('Sweet Faustus, think of heaven' – Scene 5, line 20), and by the Old Man again and again (Scene 12) as he tries to remind Faustus of his Christian potential. 'Sweet' can be appropriated by other parties, however, in an ironic transformation: in the same scene, when commanding Mephastophilis to torture the Old Man, Faustus says 'Torment, sweet friend, that base and crooked age' (Scene 12, line 66). At this point the word takes on a blasphemous quality, and Faustus's inhumanity towards the Old Man seems the more extreme because of the terms in which he expresses it.

In this narrative of rivalrous opinions, the nature of Faustus's adherence to the warring factions constitutes the plot. Here the word 'my' can signal changing loyalties. Bound to Mephastophilis and content to identify this devil as his servant and close associate, Faustus calls him 'my Mephastophilis' (Scene 5, line 206); and in Scene 12 he even sees himself as joint owner of hell: 'With greatest torments that our hell affords' (line 68). By Scene 13, however, Faustus no longer speaks abstractly of gods in general, but has transferred the possessive pronoun to a single Christian object of belief: 'my God' (line 71) and 'my Christ' (lines 73 and 74).

The narrative of *Doctor Faustus* is thus not a narrative in the conventional sense of a complex plot, but a narrative of the changing condition of the soul. Christopher Marlowe's technique for pursuing this plot is inextricably linked with his use of language.

The technique used to narrate this spiritual journey arguably requires the audience in some sense to participate in Faustus's sensations and so understand some of what he goes through. For this to work it is essential that the audience are carried away by the distractions such as the Seven Deadly Sins and Helen of Troy; and they should also be persuaded to find humour in the **low comedy**. Faustus is then likely to become a more comprehensible and human character.

This audience-identification approach, however, is just one possibility. Other approaches generate very different interpretations of the play. If, for example, the production chooses to present the low comic scenes as tawdry or even degraded, then the play will narrate the story of Faustus as nothing but folly. The audience will then remain aloof, and the damnation scene would perhaps lose much of its poignancy. This is certainly a possible approach (see also Staging), and a **Brechtian** production on these lines would have much to offer.

Dramatists through the sixteenth century had used a wide variety of **prose** and poetic patterns to structure their language: rhyming couplets, fourteen-syllabled lines ('fourteeners'), short lines such as those used by the poet John Skelton ('Skeltonics') and many more had been tried in the increasingly successful innyard theatres (see also Literary Background on Poetic Styles). Christopher Marlowe adapted the **iambic pentameter** line, already familiar from poets such as Chaucer, and combined it with **blank verse** to create a strikingly effective new way of writing. This line, with its driving five-beat rhythm, has dynamic pace, but also the capacity to sound easy and colloquial when necessary, since spoken English, broadly speaking, tends to fall into iambic patterns. The grandeur of Marlowe's line is supplied by his use of **polysyllables** within it, and by its strongly **end-stopped** character. As with any poetic structure, variations on the basic line can be made once the form is established, and this process of varying the original structure displays the writer's skill. Marlowe's blank verse iambic pentameter is the verse form that Shakespeare later took up, rendering it more fluid and flexible by reducing the end-stopping in favour of **enjambment** (the run-on line), and increasing the number of lines shared between different characters.

Christopher Marlowe also uses a rich vocabulary, characterised by extreme or **hyperbolic** language, which carries the reader or audience into an imaginary world filled out with references to myth and to the limits of geographical knowledge. He thus generates a sense both of excitement, and of the importance and dignity of his subject matter. His use of proper names – in particular elaborate and polysyllabic ones such as 'Mephastophilis' – sustains that sense of dignity, as does his highly-controlled habit of repetition. It is the combination of passion and control that mark out Marlowe's poetic achievement from those of his predecessors, an achievement which critics have described as a 'poetry of excess'. (See especially Harry Levin, *Christopher Marlowe: The Overreacher*, Faber and Faber, 1961, pp. 28–31 and 41.)

THEMES

ATHEISM

Like Marlowe himself, Faustus has been described as an atheist, and the conflict between belief and unbelief is a dominant theme in the play, permeating plot, dialogue and **imagery**. In discussing belief and its absence, atheism, a distinction needs to be made between the beliefs held by Faustus himself and those represented by the effects of the play overall.

The concept of atheism in the sixteenth century was not clear-cut, but it can be broken down into two categories: one, denying the existence of God; and the other, denying the goodness of God. At various points Faustus asserts or implies that there is no such thing as either God or heaven, for example, 'There is no chief but only Belzebub, / To whom Faustus doth dedicate himself' (Scene 3, lines 57–8). He uses the concept 'a mighty god' (Scene 1, line 62), apparently as an alternative to the Christian God. This does not make Faustus an atheist according to modern definitions, but it does in the period of the play. Faustus's ambition to become a god ('try thy brains to gain a deity' – Scene 1, line 63) marks him with the deadly sin of Pride, or **hubris**. In spite of his scepticism about God, he appears to believe that he possesses a soul, thus subscribing – in a contradictory manner – to some aspects of conventional theology but not others. Faustus's beliefs are generally unstable and shifting; this is the essence of the doubt he feels when he uses one belief and then the other, for example at Scene 5, lines 1–10:

> Now Faustus, must thou needs be damned,
> And canst thou not be saved.
> What boots it then to think of God or heaven?
> Away with such vain fancies and despair,
> Despair in God, and trust in Belzebub.
> Now go not backward: no, Faustus, be resolute;
> Why waverest thou? O, something soundeth in mine ears:
> 'Abjure this magic, turn to God again'.
> Ay, and Faustus will turn to God again.
> To God? He loves thee not

Similar feelings of doubt are expressed in the same scene at lines 177–8 ('When I behold the heavens, then I repent, / And curse thee, wicked

Mephastophilis') and the following passages to line 193. In lines 257–8 of Scene 5, he cries 'Ah Christ my Saviour, seek to save / Distressed Faustus' soul'. Even as late as Scene 12 he can still hesitate briefly before turning back to Mephastophilis (lines 53–6):

> Accursed Faustus, where is mercy now?
> I do repent, and yet I do despair:
> Hell strives with grace for conquest in my breast!
> What shall I do to shun the snares of death?

In this way, he seems to try out opinions, his mind moving like a pendulum from one to another and, like a scientific researcher, considering the consequences of each position. His response to doubt is to assert his own personal, individual courage, and this is typical of the early scenes of the play. Faustus's characteristic use of his own name instead of the personal pronoun supports his assertion of identity and strength of will. After all, anyone can use the first person pronouns 'I' and 'we', since these are shifting terms, with no fixed referent. Only Faustus's own name lays claim to a personal, independent identity. The contrary view is perhaps also tenable, namely that Faustus weakens a sense of his own identity by addressing himself from outside, as a second party in the conversation.

Faustus's disbelief in God is accompanied, for a time, by an associated disbelief in hell. Mephastophilis encourages this disbelief with the partial truth that hell is the state of mind of a being without God: 'For I am damned, and am now in hell' (Scene 5, line 137). To Faustus in Scene 5 this appears to be a trivial matter, but at that point, while the play still offers Faustus the possibility of repentance, he is not entirely alienated from the possibility that he may come to believe in God in time to repent. By Scene 13 this has changed: Faustus has come to believe in God, but it is apparently too late for him to repent. Thus, Scene 13 reveals that damnation and belief are actually the same thing for Faustus, since only belief brings him the understanding that generates the pain of damnation.

In presenting the idea that belief and repentance can come too late, the play itself appears to deny the doctrine of God's absolute goodness. In his last hour, Faustus sees an angry and unforgiving God, who is as controlled by the twenty-four year time structure as Faustus.

This **paradoxical** image of a God who is both in control of all things, and yet not in control because he (like anyone else) must keep his contractual obligations, can be problematic – this is one of the reasons why *Doctor Faustus* has been viewed as promoting atheism. More recently, McAlindon (1995) has argued that the image of the angry God is an attack on the unforgiving harshness of contemporary Christian theology ('*Dr Faustus*: The Predestination Theory', *English Studies* 76, pp. 215–20).

Body and soul: the elements

The contrast between the body and the soul is registered in *Doctor Faustus* in terms of a consistent collection of images, in which the body is part of the material, earthly world as opposed to the airy qualities attributed to the soul.

The earth is seen both literally and **metaphorically** as the domain of the Devil, a representation which is coherent with its position in the medieval theory of the four **elements** and their properties. For example, Valdes and Cornelius require a knowledge of minerals – mined from the earth – for conjuring, while Mephastophilis can give Faustus ample geographical information, and can conjure the images of the long-buried dead. When Faustus wishes to hide from God, he calls on the earth to open ('Earth, gape!', Scene 13, line 82) and mountains to cover him ('Mountains and hills, come, come and fall on me, / And hide me from the heavy wrath of God', Scene 13, lines 78–9). Instead, it is hell that opens: 'Ugly hell gape not!' (Scene 13, line 114). The earth, materiality and the body are part of the same **metaphoric** cluster, a metaphor originating in the idea of Adam's body being created out of earth, while the soul is breathed in by God. It is the body that requires food, hence the recurrence of eating as an accompaniment to many of Faustus's devilish activities: he dines with Valdes and Cornelius; throws the Pope's food about; and supplies grapes to the Duchess of Vanholt. Faustus's own body is even used for part of the trick on the horse-courser in Scene 10.

With the soul as the breath of God, one would expect it to be associated with air. Christopher Marlowe typically also uses 'the heavens', meaning the upper reaches above the earth, as the binary opposite of the earth, thus creating a cluster of images around the soul, air, the heavens and height. The devils (and Faustus when he is with them) have an ambiguous and corrupting relationship with the element of air. For example, Faustus can travel through air, if pulled by dragons (Chorus 2); while the air that he asks to conceal and consume him in Scene 13 (lines 85–6) is a particularly foul and earthy cloud – scarcely air at all. Devils can only acknowledge the heavens in the form of astrology, which in its turn denies theological doctrine: a property of astrology is predestination, which contradicts the doctrine of free will, by which human beings are considered to make their own moral choices.

STAGING

With such a highly **symbolic** and non-realistic play as *Doctor Faustus*, there are possibilities for a wide variety of different kinds of staging. **Allegorical** characters and shows of devils dancing make this a richly theatrical play with spectacular effects, and it is well worth trying to see as many productions as possible. Bevington & Rasmussen describe a number of modern productions in their introduction to the Revels Plays edition of *Doctor Faustus* (Manchester University Press, 1993).

Originally, *Doctor Faustus* was probably designed for a Shakespearean type of stage, with a large so-called 'thrust stage' projecting into the open-air auditorium in such a way that the members of the audience could be very close to it and feel involved in the action (see also Narrative Technique). This kind of stage is described in detail in Glynne Wickham *Early English Stages 1300–1660* (Routledge & Kegan Paul, 1963, 3 vols), Volume 2: 1576–1660, Part I; see especially Chapters 5 and 6, pp. 153–244. A full-size replica of Shakespeare's Globe theatre – very like the acting space on which *Doctor Faustus* would have appeared – has been constructed on London's South Bank, and students interested in theatre history might well pay it a visit. If the A-text was prepared for a travelling company, as some scholars suggest, then the venues available to them would have been fairly basic. They may have included open-air venues, civic halls and the halls or courtyards of pubs, all of which are known to have been used for theatrical performances in the latter part of the sixteenth century. Most of these locations tend to create an informal, spontaneous atmosphere with the audience positioned close to the players. For a modern equivalent, a **theatre-in-the-round** or a pub theatre would be very appropriate: few props would be required, and indeed a highly elaborate or realistic stage set would be undesirable, slowing down the action and the transitions between scenes. Approaches to staging also need to take into account issues of casting (see Characterisation).

PART FOUR

Textual analysis

TEXT 1   (SCENE 5, LINES 20–85)

This extract is from Scene 5, where the Good and Evil Angels appear for the first time. Faustus performs the crucial deed of signing the contract with the Devil through the intermediary of his representative, Mephastophilis. It begins the pattern in which Faustus ignores the warning signs that he is offered and fails to think logically about the consequences of his actions, because he does not analyse Mephastophilis's answers correctly.

GOOD ANGEL
>   Sweet Faustus, think of heaven, and heavenly things.

EVIL ANGEL
>   No Faustus, think of honour and of wealth.

>   *Exeunt* [ANGELS]

FAUSTUS
>   Of wealth!
>   Why, the signory of Emden shall be mine
>   When Mephastophilis shall stand by me.
>   What god can hurt thee, Faustus? Thou art safe,
>   Cast no more doubts. Come Mephastophilis,
>   And bring glad tidings from great Lucifer.
>   Is't not midnight? Come Mephastophilis:
>   *Veni, veni Mephastophile.*

>   *Enter* MEPHASTOPHILIS

>   Now tell me, what says Lucifer thy lord?

MEPHASTOPHILIS
>   That I shall wait on Faustus whilst he lives,
>   So he will buy my service with his soul.

FAUSTUS
>   Already Faustus hath hazarded that for thee.

MEPHASTOPHILIS

But Faustus, thou must bequeath it solemnly,

And write a deed of gift with thine own blood,

For that security craves great Lucifer.

If thou deny it, I will back to hell.

FAUSTUS

Stay Mephastophilis, and tell me,

What good will my soul do thy lord?

MEPHASTOPHILIS

Enlarge his kingdom.

FAUSTUS

Is that the reason he tempts us thus?

MEPHASTOPHILIS

Solamen miseris socios habuisse doloris.

FAUSTUS

Have you any pain that torture others?

MEPHASTOPHILIS

As great as have the human souls of men.

But tell me Faustus, shall I have thy soul?

And I will be thy slave and wait on thee,

And give thee more than thou hast wit to ask.

FAUSTUS

Ay Mephastophilis, I give it thee.

MEPHASTOPHILIS

Then stab thine arm courageously,

And bind thy soul, that at some certain day

Great Lucifer may claim it as his own,

And then be thou as great as Lucifer.

FAUSTUS

Lo Mephastophilis, for love of thee,

I cut mine arm, and with my proper blood

Assure my soul to be great Lucifer's,

Chief lord and regent of perpetual night.

View here the blood that trickles from mine arm,

And let it be propitious for my wish.

MEPHASTOPHILIS

But Faustus, thou must write it

In manner of a deed of gift.

FAUSTUS

Ay, so I will; but Mephastophilis,

My blood congeals and I can write no more.

MEPHASTOPHILIS

I'll fetch thee fire to dissolve it straight.

Exit

FAUSTUS

What might the staying of my blood portend?

Is it unwilling I should write this bill?

Why streams it not, that I may write afresh:

'Faustus gives to thee his soul': ah, there it stayed!

Why should'st thou not? Is not thy soul thine own?

Then write again: 'Faustus gives to thee his soul'.

Enter MEPHASTOPHILIS *with a chafer of coals*

MEPHASTOPHILIS

Here's fire, come Faustus, set it on.

FAUSTUS

So, now the blood begins to clear again.

Now will I make an end immediately.

MEPHASTOPHILIS

O what will not I do to obtain his soul!

FAUSTUS

Consummatum est, this bill is ended,

And Faustus hath bequeathed his soul to Lucifer.

But what is this inscription on mine arm?

Homo fuge. Whither should I fly?

If unto God, he'll throw thee down to hell;

My senses are deceived, here's nothing writ;

I see it plain, here in this place is writ,

Homo fuge! Yet shall not Faustus fly.

MEPHASTOPHILIS

I'll fetch him somewhat to delight his mind.

Exit

Enter [again] with DEVILS, *giving crowns and rich apparel to* FAUSTUS; *they dance, and then depart*

FAUSTUS

Speak Mephastophilis, what means this show?

MEPHASTOPHILIS

Nothing Faustus, but to delight thy mind withal,

And to show thee what magic can perform.

This scene sees the first appearance of the most clearly allegorical figures in the play, the Good and Evil Angels. Even though they have relatively few lines, *Doctor Faustus* is renowned for these figures since they strike those critics who have naturalistic expectations of theatre as extraordinary. They speak directly to Faustus, uttering clear, simple statements of their diametrically opposed positions. These stichomythic exchanges make no pretence of realism: they are an overtly poetic construct, and highly effective dramatically. Their speeches create a pause in the action, during which the audience can reflect on the moral situation. They do not formulate arguments; rather, they make assertions and definitions. They therefore do not function within a humanist discourse (see Historical Background) of logical debate – a world which Faustus inhabits and which he believes himself to control. Instead they use the discourse of faith, where Faustus is incompetent. He must believe one or the other, and solves that problem by echoing the last speaker.

A tendency on Faustus's part to read incorrectly appears here, as it does at other points in the play (e.g. Scene 2, where Faustus reads out inadequate portions of the texts he consults). 'Read' should be taken in its broadest sense, in addition to the literal meaning of reading printed words, to include interpretation of another person's words, of symbols, and even of situations. In this extract, Faustus is in fact faced with all of these in turn: spoken words; symbols; written words; and situation.

Faustus apparently fails to even hear the first spoken words in this extract – the warning words of the Good Angel – and he interprets the Evil Angel's words to suit himself. Later, when Mephastophilis says 'And I will be thy slave and wait on thee, / And give thee more than thou hast wit to ask' (lines 46–7), Faustus hears the promise of line 46, but misses the stinging ambiguity of Mephastophilis's sophistry in line 47: receiving more than he has 'wit to ask' could, logically, still be very little, if the person asking is stupid. Faustus is so confident of his own intelligence ('wit') and imagination that he believes Mephastophilis has promised a great deal. The common modern phrase 'he got more than he bargained for' contains the same implication that 'more' might actually be worse: in Faustus's case it could be the full experience of hell.

The **symbol** of the congealing blood is correctly read at first, as 'unwilling' to cooperate in the contract – the body somehow knows better than the mind. Faustus answers the body with a **rhetorical question,** assuming the answer 'yes': 'Is not thy soul thine own?' (line 68). He thus ignores the symbolic message offered by his own blood, that giving away his soul is an unnatural act precisely because the soul is his own and cannot rightly be someone else's.

A second symbol in this extract is the dance by the devils, brought by Mephastophilis to distract Faustus from the importance of his commitment. The devils flatter Faustus by giving him 'crowns' (signifying political power) and 'rich apparel' (signifying wealth and luxury). The dance delights his senses, and perhaps also his mind, and the whole display is intended as a promise to Faustus of things to come. It is also a diversion, in that it prevents Faustus from thinking clearly about the consequences of his actions. Faustus admits that he does not understand it when he asks Mephastophilis what the show means, and naïvely accepts Mephastophilis's answer unquestioningly. Mephastophilis both lies and tells the truth in line 84: the show is 'to delight thy mind', yet it does not mean 'nothing'. Like all the devilish shows in the play, an underlying meaning is that the devil can control appearances but not truth (or spiritual reality), and can only function by preventing people from considering moral issues carefully.

Although Faustus signs the contract at this point, it is not clear whether he has written it himself, or whether 'write' in this context means something more restricted such as 'sign'. If the latter is the case, he seems not to read it until later in the scene: an excessively trusting habit. The only written words Faustus actually reads aloud at this point are in the warning phrase '*Homo fuge*' ('flee, man'), which appears miraculously on his arm. Faustus's first reaction is to believe that he is imagining it: 'My senses are deceived' (line 79). That is, he disbelieves in God, who is the only possible author of these words. When the words insist, by repeating themselves, he still refuses to believe their message. Illogically, he asserts that God would not accept him anyway – but does not ask why else God would have sent the words. He faces them with his typical response to doubt: grim determination.

More fundamental still is Faustus's failure to interpret accurately the situation in which he is placing himself. This is perhaps the single most important issue of the play. When Faustus says 'the signory of Emden shall be mine / When Mephastophilis shall stand by me' (lines 23–4), he utters a truth, but interprets this glory as a result of his own absolute power. Clearly it is not, for he requires Mephastophilis's assistance. Even his power over Mephastophilis is limited, for Mephastophilis is controlled by Lucifer and obeys Faustus only because Lucifer has instructed him to do so. Faustus's interpretation of lines 23–4 follows as an implied **generalisation**: 'What god can hurt thee, Faustus?' – another **rhetorical question**, assuming the answer 'none'. Here he is wrong. The kind of worldly power Mephastophilis can help him to acquire has nothing to do with the moral power that would protect him from divine retribution. His conclusion, addressing himself, is 'Thou art safe' (line 25), a considerable misreading of his situation. When Faustus addresses Mephastophilis with 'what says Lucifer thy lord?' (line 30), that very need to enquire emblematises his submission into the hierarchy of hell. It shows the audience the contradiction between what Faustus thinks he is doing and what he is really getting himself into.

Finally, Faustus again fails to interpret his situation correctly when he believes Mephastophilis's assumption that the contract is final and binding, as a 'normal' contract on earth would be. On many occasions in the play Faustus is offered the opportunity to break the contract, and he refuses to do so, apparently believing a breach to be impossible. This has its own illogicality, since theologically Faustus is already abrogating the Christian contract whereby Christ was seen as having 'bought' the souls of all people in exchange for his death on the cross. Hence such colloquial phrases as 'we owe God a death' and 'by Christ that me bought', which were in common use in the sixteenth century, do not occur in *Doctor*

Faustus. This abrogation does not cross Faustus's mind, due to his failure of understanding.

TEXT 2   (SCENE 10, LINES 1–62)

This scene of **low comedy**, from the middle section of the play, is one of the scenes which used to be disregarded in discussions of *Doctor Faustus*, and even sometimes omitted from productions. More recently critics have tended to look closely at the low comedy scenes, to see how they reflect on the more intense episodes. Several topics are of interest: the plot (and its treatment of contracts); the use of prose and verse; the position of Mephastophilis; and the body.

Enter [to them] a HORSE-COURSER

HORSE-COURSER

I have been all this day seeking one Master Fustian: 'mass, see where he is! God save you, master doctor.

FAUSTUS

What, horse-courser: you are well met.

HORSE-COURSER

Do you hear, sir; I have brought you forty dollars for your horse.

FAUSTUS

I cannot sell him so: if thou lik'st him for fifty, take him.

HORSE-COURSER

Alas sir, I have no more. I pray you speak for me.

MEPHASTOPHILIS

I pray you let him have him; he is an honest fellow, and he has a great charge – neither wife nor child.

FAUSTUS

Well; come, give me your money; my boy will deliver him to you. But I must tell you one thing before you have him: ride him not into the water at any hand.

HORSE-COURSER

Why sir, will he not drink of all waters?

FAUSTUS

O yes, he will drink of all waters, but ride him not into the water. Ride him over
hedge or ditch, or where thou wilt, but not into the water.

HORSE-COURSER

Well sir. Now am I made man for ever: I'll not leave my horse for forty! If he
had but the quality of hey ding ding, hey ding ding, I'd make a brave living on
him! He has a buttock as slick as an eel. Well, God b'y sir; your boy will deliver
him me. But hark ye sir, if my horse be sick, or ill at ease, if I bring his water to
you, you'll tell me what it is?

Exit HORSE-COURSER

FAUSTUS

Away, you villain! What, dost think I am a horse-doctor?
What art thou, Faustus, but a man condemned to die?
Thy fatal time doth draw to final end.
Despair doth drive distrust unto my thoughts:
Confound these passions with a quiet sleep.
Tush, Christ did call the thief upon the cross;
Then rest thee, Faustus, quiet in conceit.

Sleep in his chair

Enter HORSE-COURSER *all wet, crying*

HORSE-COURSER

Alas, alas, Doctor Fustian, quoth 'a: 'mass, Doctor Lopus was never such a
doctor! H'as given me a purgation, h'as purged me of forty dollars! I shall never
see them more. But yet, like an ass as I was, I would not be ruled by him; for he
bade me I should ride him into no water. Now I, thinking my horse had had
some rare quality that he would not have had me known of, I, like a vent'rous
youth, rid him into the deep pond at the town's end. I was no sooner in the
middle of the pond, but my horse vanished away, and I sat upon a bottle of hay,
never so near drowning in my life! But I'll seek out my doctor, and have my
forty dollars again, or I'll make it the dearest horse. O, yonder is his snipper-
snapper! Do you hear, you hey-pass, where's your master?

MEPHASTOPHILIS

Why sir, what would you? You cannot speak with him.

HORSE-COURSER

But I will speak with him.

MEPHASTOPHILIS

Why, he's fast asleep; come some other time.

HORSE-COURSER

I'll speak with him now, or I'll break his glass-windows about his ears.

MEPHASTOPHILIS

I tell thee, he has not slept this eight nights.

HORSE-COURSER

And he has not slept this eight weeks I'll speak with him.

MEPHASTOPHILIS

See where he is, fast asleep.

HORSE-COURSER

Ay, this is he; God save ye master doctor, master doctor, master Doctor Fustian, forty dollars, forty dollars for a bottle of hay.

MEPHASTOPHILIS

Why, thou seest he hears thee not.

HORSE-COURSER

So ho ho; so ho ho.

                     Halloo in his ear ·

No, will you not wake? I'll make you wake ere I go.

                     Pull him by the leg, and pull it away

Alas, I am undone! What shall I do?

FAUSTUS

O my leg, my leg! Help, Mephastophilis! Call the officers! My leg, my leg!

MEPHASTOPHILIS

Come villain, to the constable.

HORSE-COURSER

O lord, sir! Let me go, and I'll give you forty dollars more.

This comic scene echoes the main plot but with some differences. The horse-courser is very keen to buy the 'horse' from Faustus, who has deceived him into believing that a bundle of hay is a valuable animal. This structure mirrors Faustus's own desire to buy magical knowledge from Mephastophilis and Lucifer, and his self-deception in believing such magic to be worth what he is willing to pay. The idea of a contract as an area of instability and even of some danger is present here, for the horse-courser was 'never so near drowning in my life'. The horse-courser cannot win in this situation, for when he complains about the deal, Faustus and

Mephastophilis manage to blackmail him out of even more money. Similarly, Faustus's weak attempts at repentance are thwarted in other areas of the play, and both Faustus and the horse-courser find that their own fear of the law (in Faustus's case the law of God; in the horse-courser's the criminal law) prevents them from pursuing the matter further.

The scene uses **prose** almost throughout, an indication that it is intended to be comic. In general, the **convention** of the Elizabethan theatre was that noble and dignified events and thoughts were best expressed in verse, while prose should be used for undignified and everyday speech. This decorum is fairly clearly marked in *Doctor Faustus*. The fact that scenes with nobility, such as the Emperor (Scene 9) and the Duke and Duchess of Vanholt (Scene 11), are in prose suggests that Faustus's achievements in those scenes are also petty and meretricious.

Faustus returns to **blank verse** at lines 25–9, where he muses to himself on the most serious matter of all: what will happen to him after death? He notices that his life will soon be over, and experiences a sense of **despair**. Characteristically, he tries to avoid thinking about the problem by going to sleep – the effect of this is similar to the tactic of distraction practised on him in Scene 5 by the dance of devils and again by the parade of the Seven Deadly Sins. He does not fall asleep immediately, and in line 28 he draws comfort from the possibility of forgiveness, but without actually repenting. He reasons that if Christ forgave the thief on the cross beside him, then Faustus, another sinner, might also be forgiven.

Blank verse is an ideally economical medium in which to display the lucid articulation of Faustus's thoughts, and the uneasy toing and froing of his mind. Each sentence is neat, complete and closed off by the **end-stopped** lines; each new line gives Faustus's thoughts a new direction, until he finally falls asleep. The last word leaves the audience with an unresolved ambiguity: 'quiet in conceit' may mean 'peaceful with this thought' or 'peaceful in this proud delusion'. The former interpretation implies that Faustus will repent in time to obtain salvation, the latter that he won't. Faustus may sleep peacefully, but the audience is left with an itch of uncertainty – an **aporia**. From that the audience shares the experience Faustus has had on earlier occasions, that of distraction, when the next focus is not on the serious problem, but on the ridiculous horse-courser's antics.

In this scene, as in Scenes 7, 9 and 11, Mephastophilis has become a willing confederate in Faustus's pranks. This is neither the servile, inhuman devil that we met in Scene 3, nor the sadistic torturer of Scenes 12 and 13, but a cooperative companion who helps the joke along and participates in its payoff. (It is Mephastophilis who stings the horse-courser with the demand for an extra forty dollars.) In addition, Mephastophilis speaks very adequate colloquial prose through these scenes. This change in Mephastophilis might be interpreted in several ways, as:

- dramatically convenient, to give Faustus a 'friend'
- a sign that Faustus is degenerating, as he chooses devilish rather than human company
- a poignant attempt by Mephastophilis to try out the simple pleasures of human company for a time, before reverting to type in Scene 12.

The first time one sees the episode of the detachable leg performed, it can come as a considerable shock (if it is effectively staged). The act of dismemberment foreshadows Faustus's torments in hell, which are becoming more and more likely. When it becomes clear (later in the scene, after the end of this extract) that the leg was a magically-contrived fake, it seems that Faustus is in control again, but he is still only in control of the body: of physical as opposed to spiritual matters. This is a permanent feature of the kind of magic he has 'bought' with his soul: that it is always on a physical level. He cannot change the nature of things but only their appearances – the bottle of hay reverts; the grapes in Scene 11 must be fetched from a distance; Helen of Troy (Scene 12) is a performance by a devil; and so on. Thus Faustus resembles the horse-courser, in that he has bought an illusion (in Faustus's case, of power) and not the thing itself.

TEXT 3   (SCENE 13, LINES 59–115)

This extract from Scene 13 must stand as one of the most impressive and moving passages in the theatrical tradition. Faustus, isolated from human companionship and alone on stage till the last three lines, moves through the final hour of his life in a condition of intense feeling and anguished thought, expressed in graphic **imagery** of awesome magnitude. Finally his reasoning capacities are clear, and are related to the reality of his spiritual circumstances. The question of belief is now taken for granted: since hearing the Old Man's words in Scene 12, Faustus no longer questions the existence of God, or of hell. At last he comes to see himself not as Faustus the exceptional being, but as simply the bearer of a human soul. Facing damnation, he reasons with himself accordingly.

The clock strikes eleven

FAUSTUS

> Ah Faustus,
> Now hast thou but one bare hour to live,
> And then thou must be damned perpetually.
> Stand still, you ever-moving spheres of heaven,
> That time may cease, and midnight never come.
> Fair Nature's eye, rise, rise again, and make
> Perpetual day, or let this hour be but
> A year, a month, a week, a natural day,
> That Faustus may repent and save his soul.
> *O lente, lente currite noctis equi!*
> The stars move still, time runs, the clock will strike,
> The devil will come, and Faustus must be damned.
> O I'll leap up to my God! Who pulls me down?
> See, see where Christ's blood streams in the firmament!
> One drop would save my soul, half a drop: ah my Christ –
> Ah, rend not my heart for naming of my Christ;
> Yet will I call on him – O spare me, Lucifer!
> Where is it now? 'Tis gone: and see where God
> Stretcheth out his arm, and bends his ireful brows!
> Mountains and hills, come, come and fall on me,
> And hide me from the heavy wrath of God.
> No, no?
> Then will I headlong run into the earth:
> Earth, gape! O no, it will not harbour me.

You stars that reigned at my nativity,
Whose influence hath allotted death and hell,
Now draw up Faustus like a foggy mist
Into the entrails of yon labouring cloud,
That when you vomit forth into the air
My limbs may issue from your smoky mouths,
So that my soul may but ascend to heaven.

The watch strikes

Ah, half the hour is past: 'twill all be past anon.
O God, if thou wilt not have mercy on my soul,
Yet for Christ's sake, whose blood hath ransomed me,
Impose some end to my incessant pain:
Let Faustus live in hell a thousand years,
A hundred thousand, and at last be saved.
O, no end is limited to damned souls!
Why wert thou not a creature wanting soul?
Or why is this immortal that thou hast?
Ah, Pythagoras' *metempsychosis* – were that true,
This soul should fly from me, and I be changed
Unto some brutish beast:
All beasts are happy, for when they die,
Their souls are soon dissolved in elements;
But mine must live still to be plagued in hell.
Cursed be the parents that engendered me:
No Faustus, curse thy self, curse Lucifer,
That hath deprived thee of the joys of heaven!

The clock striketh twelve

O it strikes, it strikes! Now body, turn to air,
Or Lucifer will bear thee quick to hell.

Thunder and lightning

O soul, be changed into little water drops,
And fall into the ocean, ne'er to be found.
My God, my God, look not so fierce on me!

Enter DEVILS

Adders and serpents, let me breathe awhile!
Ugly hell gape not! Come not, Lucifer!
I'll burn my books – ah, Mephastophilis!

Exeunt with him

Time is a fundamental aspect of the play. Much of this monologue is concerned with the passage of time, which Faustus counts out by the stars and the sun. The external sound of the clock striking imposes the idea that time is out of his control: the clock is almost certainly a church clock, and need not be on stage. Faustus considers for a moment the idea that it is the movement of the stars that creates time, and so he can make time stop if he can make them stand still (line 62) or make the sun rise (line 64). The sun and stars are located in the heavens, and so outside the sphere of his control, since his power is limited to what the earth-bound Mephastophilis can do. Thus time, Faustus's enemy, must move forward. It is God who determines how long the whole of human time will run by choosing the Day of Judgement, and who presides over the concept of eternity. When Faustus next thinks of time it is indeed of eternity: the eternity that he will spend in hell. For the first time in the play he begins to have an imaginative idea of what this might mean, and counts out huge spaces of time ('a thousand years, / A hundred thousand', lines 94–5) which are still less than eternity, in order to beg to spend only that long in torment. When even this is apparently impossible, and when he fully understands what is happening, the monologue ends, midnight strikes and the devils remove him.

One dramatic effect of placing such a long speech at the end of the play is to build up tension, and the audience's desire to be released from tension: it can actually be painful to witness Faustus's drawn-out mental anguish and desperate search for alternatives. When the devils finally appropriate him, the audience feels a sense of release and relief – they, at least, need not continue to share Faustus's tortured state. A strong sense of having escaped is part of the experience of watching and listening to *Doctor Faustus*, and perhaps also part of its educative aim.

The **imagery** of the passage systematically concludes the use of the images which have dominated the play. The motif of the four **elements** (see Themes) is encountered again when the heavy earth of the mountains and hills (which will not save his body), the vapours of the clouds (which are a kind of hellish version of air rather than the air itself, which is the heavenly medium) and the water drops (where Faustus equally fruitlessly wishes his soul could dissolve) are all contrasted with the saving grace of the blood of Christ. Thus Faustus lists earth, water and air. Fire is unmentioned, because in its literal form it exists in hell. Imagery of height and depth continues, for Faustus sees heaven as something he will leap up to, and Lucifer as dragging him back down to the earth. Faustus at last longs for heaven and forgiveness but when he comes to repent he is now so given over to the Devil that he has not the strength of will to ignore Lucifer's physical assaults on his body, a failing noticeably contrary to the example of Christian endurance offered by the Old Man in Scene 12.

The verse of this extract offers one of the most poignant lines in poetry: 'See, see where Christ's blood streams in the firmament!' (line 72), recalling the congealed blood which would not 'stream' when Faustus signed his soul away in Scene 5. The flowing verse of this line is then followed by a series of fragmented thoughts, often in part-lines. Faustus first addresses these to himself: 'One drop would save my soul'; then to Christ: 'ah my Christ'; then to Lucifer: 'Ah, rend not my heart for naming of my Christ'; to himself again: 'Yet will I call on him'; before (fatally) turning back to Lucifer: 'O spare me, Lucifer!' After this climactic indecision, Faustus discovers that the vision of grace has vanished – instead he is shortly to see (or imagine) an angry, punitive God.

In the course of the speech, the concept of a unified identity, an 'I' who wishes to hide from God under mountains or in the earth, is analysed and perceived to be a separable body and soul. Faustus also accepts the theological definition of the human soul as immortal. It is not the body that will suffer in hell, but the soul. And this is, in a way, the most extreme aspect of the trick that has been played on Faustus – that the pleasures he gained were of the body, yet the soul must suffer to pay for them.

PART FIVE

Background

AUTHOR AND WORKS

Christopher Marlowe was born in 1564 in Canterbury, Kent and died of a knife wound in Deptford, London on 30 May 1593. A description of his life can read almost like a work of fiction, with its dramatic moments, its sense of mystery, and its violent early end (see also Chronology). Scholars have been fascinated by Marlowe's life, and documents relating to it continue to be discovered. At this point in time, over four hundred years since his death, much of what is suggested about him involves speculation and interpretation.

Christopher Marlowe's father was a cobbler, a relatively badly paid profession; but even so Marlowe was well educated, attending first the King's School, Canterbury and going on to university studies at Corpus Christi College, Cambridge. Much of the curriculum at Cambridge at that time involved the intensive study of theology and of ancient languages. This academic background infuses the whole atmosphere and style of debate in *Doctor Faustus*, and informs the scenes where the scholars appear. While still a student at Cambridge, Marlowe travelled abroad on Government business, from which information scholars conclude that he was probably spying for Sir Francis Walsingham's secret service. In particular he may have infiltrated the (Catholic) Jesuit community at Rheims in France. This could be consistent with the idea that he was a member of the puritan movement, and followed its emphasis on free speech. Alternatively, it is also speculated that Marlowe may have become a Catholic sympathiser and a double agent while in France. (See Historical Background.) This is not as improbable as it might seem, since both the state and powerful members of the nobility certainly did run spy networks throughout the Tudor period, which was fraught with both foreign wars and internal dissent. Marlowe's own contribution to this is probable rather than proven. Especially interesting reading on this topic is Charles Nicholl's *The Reckoning: The Murder of Christopher Marlowe* (Jonathan Cape, 1992).

Marlowe left Cambridge for London in 1587 and took up the profession of **playwright**, at which he was immediately successful with *Tamburlaine the Great* and its sequel, *Tamburlaine the Great, Part II*. The hero of these plays is a bloodthirsty tyrant, and audiences flocked to see the spectacular battle scenes, and to hear the blood-curdling poetry in the grand style with which Tamburlaine conducted politics as slaughter. Tamburlaine foreshadows Faustus in his overweening pride and ambition, and his **ambivalent** relationship with God.

The dates of composition of Marlowe's plays are not absolutely certain, and he may have begun writing while still at university. *Dido, Queen of Carthage* probably dates from this early period, followed by the two parts of *Tamburlaine*. *Doctor Faustus* was probably written next, in the late 1580s, followed by a masterpiece of black humour, *The Jew of Malta*. Last came the less well-known story of Huguenot persecution, *The Massacre at Paris*, and the history play, *Edward II*, narrating the reign, deposition and murder of that king. It has been suggested that *Doctor Faustus* was not written until 1592, when an English translation of the German stories about Faustus was available (see Literary Background). This date seems less likely nowadays than one of around 1588, as evidence of earlier editions of the stories has come to light. In addition to the plays, Christopher Marlowe wrote lyric poetry; translated Ovid's *Amores* (from which comes the line '*O lente, lente currite noctis equi!*' – *Doctor Faustus*, Scene 13, line 68); translated Lucan's *Pharsalia*; and composed *Hero and Leander*, an **epyllion** of great charm.

Christopher Marlowe's lifestyle in London after leaving university was that of a single young man who lived amongst a crowd of similar friends, including the playwright Thomas Kyd. Making money as and where he could, Marlowe's contacts included intellectuals, con-men and spies. While he is reported to have spent time in serious conversations about religion, he also fell foul of the law over brawls on two occasions: in 1589 and in 1592. He also had powerful political connections, including the spymaster and Secretary of State to Queen Elizabeth I, Sir Francis Walsingham, and his brother Sir Thomas Walsingham.

At the time of Marlowe's death, and shortly afterwards, some contemporaries claimed that Marlowe expressed atheistic and seditious views. Richard Baines, a Government informer, wrote that 'almost into every company he cometh he persuades men to Atheism, willing them not to be afeared of bugbears and hobgoblins, and utterly scorning both god and his ministers.' Baines claimed that Marlowe asserted that 'all they that love not tobacco and boys were fools.' Thomas Kyd, while under arrest, also made accusations against Marlowe. We cannot take this so-called evidence as straightforward truth, as it is hearsay and could well have been invented by enemies who wished to discredit Marlowe and his friends. Suspicion of atheism has clung to Marlowe's reputation over the centuries, and has led some readers to interpret the character of Faustus as a version of Marlowe himself. J.B. Steane, for example, argues for a strong intellectual relationship between Marlowe and his creation, in his introduction to *Christopher Marlowe: the Complete Plays* (Penguin, 1969, p. 16):

> It was a very individual mind that created as he created: and what we see as we read is a whole mind involved, not simply or primarily the craftsman's concern with techniques, like a shoemaker's, or a professional rhetorician's. Moreover Marlowe concerned himself recurrently with certain ideas, feelings and aspects of life: these were what interested him .... It must also be recognised that it is a possible but not inevitable source of distorted judgement on the work.

Such a move lacks reasonable foundation: all that can fairly be said is that the play's subject matter is the exploration of problems of belief, and that the conclusion drawn is not necessarily atheistic. God may be terrifying – and even vindictive – in this play, but he certainly exists.

It is possible that Marlowe's death, whether brought about by self-defence or murder, was connected with Baines's accusations and the scandal which was about to emerge. Marlowe was invited to a meal at an eating-house in Deptford, at the end of which he was dead from a knife-wound to the eye. The two witnesses related a story of a quarrel and a scuffle between Marlowe and a man named Ingram Frizar, during which this nasty 'accident' occurred, and the coroner was satisfied. Scholars such as Leslie Hotson and Charles Nicholl have been rather more suspicious, seeing Marlowe's death and the subsequent tarnishing of his reputation as altogether too convenient. J.B. Steane (ibid.) puts the opposite view for seeing these reports of Marlowe as possibly exaggerated, but having some basis in fact:

As for Marlowe the man, atheist and rebel or not, we have to acknowledge
that there is no single piece of evidence that is not hearsay – only that there is a
good deal of it, that it is reasonably consistent, and that on the other side there
is no single fact or piece of hearsay known to us that will rank as evidence against
it.

An output of seven major plays in around six years was sufficient to give
Marlowe an impressive place amongst the most highly-regarded
dramatists. His tragically early death at the age of twenty-nine no doubt
deprived literature of even greater and more developed works. As Simon
Shepherd puts it in his introduction to *Marlowe and the Politics of
Elizabethan Theatre* (Harvester, Brighton, 1984, p. xiii): 'I would suggest
that had he lived Marlowe might well have produced a set of texts of an
artistic quality that would rival if not excel Shakespeare's.'

Literary background

The Faust story

Much of the information in *Doctor Faustus* is derived from a collection of
stories in German called the *Faustbuch* ('Faust Book'). Marlowe almost
certainly did not read German and relied on an English translation by
P.F. (full name unknown) titled *The Historie of the Damnable Life, and
Deserved Death of Doctor John Faustus*. The earliest known edition of the
English version dates from 1592, but it is possible that Marlowe read
another edition (now lost) as early as 1587, while he was still at
Cambridge. The stories in the *Faustbuch* narrate in **prose** the semi-
mythical tales which built up around a real-life German scholar and
travelling magician, Georgius of Helmstadt, also known as Georgius
Faustus. Christopher Marlowe's play selects heavily, cutting or reporting
those stories which were too grandiose to show on stage, and finds ways
to fit twenty-four years of life into a play of about two hours' duration (see
Critical Approaches on Time). In general, Marlowe adheres quite closely
to the three-part structure of the *Faustbuch*:
- a contract with the Devil and research into cosmology and geography
- miraculous travels and displays of conjuring
- death, regret and damnation.

When the play was rewritten and expanded to form the B-text (see Note on the Text), additional episodes of magic from the *Faustbuch* were inserted in the middle section, but the three-part structure was retained.

Marlowe transformed the naïve stories from the *Faustbuch* by giving Faustus a voice with which he could examine his own state of mind and think through moral problems in detail (see Historical Background on Humanism). Where the *Faustbuch* narrates a simple tale of wickedness and well-deserved punishment, Marlowe creates a **tragedy** in which a human being makes a clear choice for more or less understandable reasons, and with some knowledge of the possible consequences. A number of artists have since presented interpretations of the Faust story, notably the German poet, dramatist and novelist Johann Wolfgang von Goethe, in his plays *Faust Part I* (1808) and *Faust Part II* (1832), and the French composer Charles Gounod, in his lyric opera *Faust* (1859). Other works drawing on the story include Hector Berlioz's operatic *Damnation of Faust* (1846), Thomas Mann's novel *Doctor Faustus* (1948), and more recently a cinematic version by Czech film-maker and animator Jan Švankmajer, *Faust* (1994).

OTHER LITERARY SOURCES

More generally, the theme of the human being whose ambition and vision lead him or her to challenge or disobey a god is widespread in most cultures. Marlowe's *Doctor Faustus* derives specifically from several of these:

- the Adam and Eve myth, from the Judaeo–Christian tradition, is referred to in Scene 1 (lines 44–5): original sin is what the human race is supposed to have inherited from Adam
- the fall of Lucifer (or Satan) from heaven to hell as a punishment for wishing to be equal with God (as explained in Scene 3, lines 63–75) is presented in the Old Testament, but was even better known within popular culture of Marlowe's time as one of the **Mystery Plays**. An edition of a play of the fall of Lucifer can be found in Peter Happé (ed.), *English Mystery Plays* (Penguin, 1975)
- the Ancient Greek myth of Daedalus and Icarus, where Icarus disobeyed his father's instructions and perished because he flew too

high (Prologue, lines 20–2). The phrase 'fly too high' is often used in everyday speech as a **metaphor** for excessive ambition, like that of Faustus.

Morality plays

Many readers have noticed resemblances between *Doctor Faustus* and what is now called the **Morality Play,** a genre of theatre very popular from the early 1400s to the 1580s. Even after the 1580s many plays (through to about 1630) continued to contain references to typical Morality Play events and characters, indicating that these plays were familiar, memorable and widespread. The Morality Play is therefore a genre which makes the transition from the Medieval to the Early Modern period. This may seem surprising, and the name itself may sound misleading until one realises just how much immorality they in fact contain.

Each Morality Play follows a common basic narrative structure, with its own unique variations. The basic structure is as follows. The central character is an ordinary person – someone with whom the whole audience can identify, who has ordinary human experiences. This representative character, who is usually male, is called the **mankind figure**. He has responsibilities, works hard, feels bored, hungry and tired. At this point he is approached by a group of tempters who suggest that he should leave his responsibilities for a while and go out for a drink and perhaps a meal with them. These are the chief **Vice** and the **vice-crew**. One thing leads to another, and the mankind figure goes rapidly downhill, forgetting his work or his study, and consorting with low company. These are the most entertaining scenes of the play, and generally involve obscene jokes, tumbling, juggling, comic drunkenness, singing and general uproarious tomfoolery. The Vice's wooden sword or dagger may be much in evidence, in comic stage-business. (The heirs to this kind of performance tradition have continued to amuse modern audiences, in the form of the Marx Brothers, the Three Stooges, and similar comedians.)

From time to time virtuous and well-meaning characters approach the mankind figure to remind him of his duties and of the need to lead a virtuous life. He reforms readily, if briefly, until the vice-crew return.

More fun takes place in the form of humiliation of the virtuous characters by mocking and beating them, and sometimes putting them in the stocks. After several repetitions of the reform/relapse pattern, the mankind figure realises that he has wasted his life, and is in danger of **despair** (see Historical Background on Despair). The vice-crew offer to help him commit suicide (an act which, according to Elizabethan religious dogma, would damn his soul forever). In the nick of time, however, a virtuous adviser reappears, driving the devilish vice-crew off howling (often carrying one another piggy-back and/or vowing that they cannot be killed); the mankind figure turns joyfully to God (sometimes on his deathbed). This counts as a happy ending, whether he now dies or not, as the audience is confident that he will go to heaven.

Clearly this well-loved form had much to be said for it as pure entertainment. Facing intense criticism from moralists, acting companies justified the fun by pointing to the moral message, and saying that the display of immorality was essential, as a way of luring audiences to take in the moral content. In *The Growth and Structure of Elizabethan Comedy* (Chatto and Windus, 1952), Muriel Bradbrook explains that 'these plays are at once extremely coarse and extremely moral: scenes of good advice and of ... riot are mingled in an attempt to provide both doctrine and mirth' (p. 26).

Doctor Faustus has much in common with the Morality Plays. The narrative pattern in which a central character falls into evil ways but repeatedly considers repentance is the same. So too is the habit whereby the devils use theatrical and spectacular tactics to distract him from serious thoughts of God. The presence of evil and virtuous advisers is equally reminiscent of the Morality Plays, as is the suggestion of assisted suicide in Scene 12 (line 39 and the following stage direction):

> Damned art thou Faustus, damned; despair and die!

> MEPHASTOPHILIS *gives him a dagger*

Some of the vice pranks are **conventional**, for example in Scene 2 when Wagner hints that he may be part of the vice-crew by using a vice convention, saying 'I am by nature ... prone to lechery – to love I would say' (lines 20–1). This adjustment of the negative term 'lechery' to a euphemism is characteristic of vice behaviour. At the end of Scene 1

Marlowe mimics the stock scene in which the vice-crew lead the mankind figure to the tavern, by having Faustus withdraw with Valdes and Cornelius in order to dine.

Like the Morality Plays, *Doctor Faustus* focuses on the **dialogue** as a form of logical persuasion, an intellectual structure familiar to any student at that time. Contrary to the tradition of the Morality Plays, however, Marlowe gave most of his characters real names, and one might argue that this gives them an individuality that Morality Play characters lacked (see, however, Characterisation): characters in Morality Plays have **allegorical** names such as 'Mankind' or 'Everyman' for the mankind figure; 'Ignorance' or 'Mischief' for members of the vice-crew; and 'God's Word' or 'Mercy' for the virtuous advisers.

This close mapping of Christopher Marlowe's play onto the Morality Play **form** may prompt one to ask whether *Doctor Faustus* is in some sense unoriginal. The answer is no: like all artists, Marlowe (and his collaborator) worked within the **conventions** of the genre in a way that revised and developed them. Formal constraints need not restrict originality. Marlowe altered the Morality Play conventions to generate a radical revision of the Morality Play structure. The mankind figure was traditionally supposed to learn with age, but Faustus spectacularly fails to do so. Indeed, one of the inversions of the form is that he continues to behave like a young man (carousing and drinking with student friends) even when he is nearing death, as Wagner tells us in Chorus 4. Death and old age – the *memento mori* – were traditionally supposed to turn a person's thoughts to prayer and piety, but Faustus ostentatiously sets himself against this when he turns against the Old Man in Scene 12.

Finally, though the parallels between the Morality Plays and *Doctor Faustus* are clear, Marlowe's sophisticated version makes a striking departure from the form when his central character is not saved at the end but damned. One might say that Faustus is perhaps not representative of ordinary humanity; but it could be argued that all of us are tempted to rebel against authority at one time or another, and to see ourselves as all-important in the world, even though we do not make pacts with the Devil or attempt black magic. To that extent, at least, Faustus can be seen as a mankind figure, at the same time as he attracts our sympathy for his individualist **tragic** situation.

POETIC STYLES

Much of the sixteenth century's development of poetic and theatrical styles of writing was to do with an intersection between traditional English styles and the rediscovery of the classical traditions of Ancient Greek and Latin writing. Many writers were involved in translating or freely adapting classical material into English. In the early part of the century, court poets such as Sir Thomas Wyatt developed **sonnet** forms, inspired by the Italian poems of Petrarch. As the century progressed, some of Wyatt's freedom and flexibility was lost, as innovators used a stricter, more regular metrical form. Classical poetry had followed extremely strict rules of metre based on the lengths of syllables ('quantity') which can be rendered in the stress-based English vernacular only with some awkwardness. Nevertheless, many poets strongly defended the use of classical forms for English poetry. Some poets and playwrights used the 'fourteener', a line of fourteen syllables, which captured some of the lengthy feeling of the classical hexameter line, but was popular only for the middle part of the century. It tends to break into the rather jingling short lines of **ballad rhythm** (four stresses plus three stresses), and is still used in popular poetry today. Experiments to achieve classical effects continued throughout the sixteenth century, the most successful being the **heroic couplet**, which flourished for centuries afterwards. Among the poets who experimented with larger structures such as rhyme schemes and the form of the lyric stanza was Sir Philip Sidney, in the *Arcadia*.

In the theatre, playwrights were inspired by classical dramatists, especially Seneca, but also by English history, by legends and by stories of famous or holy people. In general, all of the rhythmic forms mentioned above were tried out in the theatre in the course of the century, with the final preference resting with iambic pentameter **blank verse** interspersed with **prose** and with some iambic pentameter **couplets** for such special effects as signalling the close of a scene. Christopher Marlowe's *Doctor Faustus* can be seen to be a part of that development, with its confident iambic pentameter blank verse, and its large-scale structures of verse paragraphs (see also Critical Approaches on Language). It also moves consistently between prose for the scenes of **low comedy** and blank verse for the more dignified and intense sequences, using the convention of poetic **decorum**.

HISTORICAL BACKGROUND

ROMAN CATHOLICISM

From the early sixteenth century Protestant Anglicanism had contended with Roman Catholicism in England, basing much of its position on the teachings of Martin Luther, and was strongly influenced by the Reformation in Northern Europe.

When *Doctor Faustus* was written, Catholicism had been banned in England since Queen Elizabeth I succeeded her sister Mary in 1558. In polemical writing and speeches the Pope was described as the Antichrist; the Catholic Church was referred to as the 'Whore of Babylon'; and Catholic forms of worship, especially the Latin Mass, were publicly reviled and feared. Various repressive laws and taxes were instituted during Elizabeth's reign to attempt to re-educate the public. War with Catholic Spain and the genuine fear of invasion (up to 1588) intensified the antipathy towards Catholicism, and recusant priests (i.e. those who did not attend Anglican services, thereby breaking the law) who were caught attempting to administer the forbidden rites could be tortured to death. Paradoxically, one of the fears relating to Catholicism was of a return to the religious executions of Queen Mary's reign. In fact, it would be difficult to say which of the two regimes was the more violent towards religious dissent. Catholicism did, however, retain its strength amongst numerous powerful families, and, as is well documented, survived in country areas including Warwickshire and Yorkshire.

Uneducated people were regularly represented on the Elizabethan stage as retaining many of their old (Catholic) traditions and oaths, perhaps realistically (in the case of those actors and playwrights who did not notice the Catholic implications), or perhaps as a deliberate attempt to mock Catholicism – some of these habits occur, for example, in the Clown scene in *Doctor Faustus*.

The religious climate has considerable relevance for *Doctor Faustus*, since Marlowe chose to place Faustus in Luther's home university of Wittenberg, thus suggesting a Protestant connection. Faustus's choice of the Pope as the butt of his **satire** and jokes (Scene 7) is also an attack on Catholicism, but with an ambiguous effect. The contemporary audience was almost certainly on Faustus's side, and ready to roar with laughter at this venal Pope's anger. On the other hand, one might think that there should come a point where Faustus's devilish connection would lose the audience's sympathy, and by implication cause the Pope to seem less laughable. That this does not happen is a logical problem: Faustus may well be puerile, but that does not save the Pope character from the audience's laughter – laughter seems to be separate from reason in the case of *Doctor Faustus*.

When Faustus uses Latin phrases to perform his conjuring, the audience might well associate this with the Latin of the Catholic Mass, and interpret the play as supporting the Elizabethan orthodoxy that Catholicism was a devilish trick. Indeed, anti-Catholic diatribes habitually described the Mass as a theatrical trick, or a conjuring trick. This skill with illusion is precisely where Lucifer and Mephastophilis are shown to excel in the play.

Putting these points together, one might reasonably conclude that *Doctor Faustus* contains a conventional Anglican attack on Roman Catholicism.

Puritans

Within the ferment of religious debate, numerous subdivisions of opinion can be traced in Elizabethan England. Mainstream Anglicanism found many of these threatening (see Catholicism above), not least the puritan sect, which advocated free speech and independence from the officially prescribed **homilies** and the orders of service of the Prayer Book devised and set down by Government decree. Instead the puritans subscribed to a tradition of preaching. They believed in individual obedience to the dictates of one's own conscience, rather than in conformity to instructions by the authorities. Naturally, the authorities found this a dangerously subversive position. Simon Shepherd (*Marlowe and the Politics of Elizabethan Theatre*, Harvester, Brighton, 1984) argues that Marlowe's plays in general and *Doctor Faustus* in particular 'often show scenes or stories in which ... individual speech is repressed or in which official speech making is viewed critically'. Shepherd interprets Faustus as struggling between an ideal of individualism as a puritan free-speaker, and the need for conformity to external structures. When Faustus obeys the last words he has heard (from the Evil Angel in Scene 5) he can be seen as parodying the establishment ideal of the obedient churchgoer.

HUMANISM

The word 'humanist' originally referred to a scholar of the Humanities, especially Classical literature. At the time of the Renaissance (around the fifteenth and sixteenth centuries) European intellectuals devoted themselves to the rediscovery and intense study of first Roman and then Greek philosophy, literature and **rhetoric**, in particular the works of Cicero, Aristotle and Plato. Out of this period of intellectual ferment there emerged a view of what it meant to be human and a philosophy quite different from medieval scholastic thinking. Reason, balance and a proper human dignity were the central ideals of humanist thought.

These concepts of the individual and of the individual conscience were developed within the education system by followers of such influential fifteenth-century Italian thinkers as Marsilio Ficino (1433–99) and Giovanni Pico della Mirandola (1463–94). Among the many humanist thinkers the Dutch priest Erasmus (?1466–1536) was particularly important: his works (in Latin) were known all over Europe. He was an independent and anti-authoritarian thinker whose criticisms of the unreformed Church paved the way for the Reformation, although he opposed Luther and the various Protestant theological factions.

As the humanists' 'new learning' spread through Europe, Erasmus was followed in sixteenth-century England by educationists and theologians, including Sir Thomas More (1478–1535) and John Colet (?1466–1519). The humanist project was to rediscover the learning of the ancient world by reviving competence in the ancient languages and reading newly discovered Latin and Greek texts. This in turn led to re-readings and re-contextualisings of familiar texts. The humanist attitude to the world was anthropocentric: instead of regarding humanity as a fallen, corrupt and sinful concept, their idea of truth and excellence was based on human values and experience. This generated conflicts with Christian religious teachings, and a conscious struggle was made to bring the ancient texts into harmony with theology (and vice versa). These theories deeply imbued the educational practices and the intellectual life of sixteenth-century England, especially in the important seats of learning: the Inns of Court, where lawyers were trained, and the universities of Oxford and Cambridge.

The humanist individual aspired to assert himself (rarely, but imaginably, herself), using the powerful intellectual tools of logic to think through concepts of theology and philosophy. Principal methods by which education took place were the public speech of persuasion and the **dialogue** – a sequence of exchanges in which two speakers argued through the opposing sides of an issue, each taking one side of the argument. Students read exemplary dialogues by writers and masters of rhetoric as well as devising their own. Thus logic, the dialogue and an adventurous mental attitude all formed part of the humanist education. These tactics are to be found in abundance in *Doctor Faustus*.

There are strong strains of the free thinker in the character of Faustus, but his version of humanism suffers from serious limitations. His intellectual ambition quickly turns into sensuality and even into a greed for power in which he envisages warlike acts (Scene 1) and eventually becomes capable of ordering the Old Man to be tortured (Scene 12).

DESPAIR

Technically, the sin of despair is defined in Christian doctrine as losing one's belief in God's capacity to forgive. In the medieval tradition it was called the 'sin against the Holy Ghost', and was considered to be the worst sin of all, because it is irrevocable. As Bevington & Rasmussen point out in their introduction to the Revels Plays edition of *Doctor Faustus* (Manchester University Press, 1993, p. 20):

> In despairing, Faustus re-enacts the crime of Judas who sinned like many a frail
> mortal in selling Christ but who refused to accept that he could be pardoned for
> his crime. And if Judas's crime of selling the Lord was forgivable, Faustus's must
> be also. His failure to repent is his supreme act of folly, certainly no less so than his
> pact with the devil.

Suicide was seen as the result of despair, which was why suicide was treated very seriously: not because it was seen as a type of murder, since that was forgivable by God, but because it indicated loss of faith in God. It could also indicate a wish to take decisions about one's life and death out of God's control – a kind of Pride. This is why Mephastophilis offers Faustus a dagger in Scene 12.

PART SIX

CRITICAL HISTORY & BROADER PERSPECTIVES

From its first performance, *Doctor Faustus* was a huge commercial and popular success, frequently revived on numerous occasions even before a printed edition of the play appeared. Financier Philip Henslowe's diary records takings in 1594 far in excess of the usual sums. Audiences particularly appreciated its exciting, rowdy qualities – apparently the devils were especially noisy and vigorous at the Fortune Theatre in the 1620s. After 1675, however, there is no recorded production until 1896, although an edition appeared in 1814. The critical tradition is a rich and extensive one, and many of the complexities of the play continue to challenge scholarship.

CONVENTIONAL APPROACHES

Following the 1814 edition, *Doctor Faustus* was treated as an example of a primitive kind of drama, the pre-Shakespearean, and denigrated for what was seen as its weak narrative construction. The poetry of the monologues and of the 'serious' portions was admired, with what John Jump calls 'indulgent sentimentalism' (p. 17 of introduction to John D. Jump (ed.), *Marlowe: Doctor Faustus*, Casebook Series, Macmillan, 1969). The temptation to compare Marlowe with Shakespeare was not resisted. This kind of response is typical of the judgemental, evaluative approach which dominated literary studies until the mid twentieth century.

Later critics questioned the justice of the final scene (Una Ellis-Fermor, 1927, reprinted in Jump, pp. 43–4) and sought an understanding of Faustus's character in the context of the history of ideas. For George Santayana (*Three Philosophical Poets*, 1910, reprinted in Jump, pp. 39–40), Faustus represented the ideal of the Renaissance free thinker, and for Henderson (*And Morning in His Eyes*, 1937, pp. 310–12, quoted in introduction to Jump, p. 15), the adventurous intellectual. These critics see Faustus as close to heroic, a true **tragic** protagonist brought down by a fatal flaw. Similar views continue to be popular, though the alternative view of Faustus as culpably foolish has gained ground – from the latter standpoint, Faustus's punishment is seen as just and the play is regarded as strongly validating Christian ideals.

A strong biographical tendency within criticism persistently links Faustus's behaviour with what little is known of Christopher Marlowe's life, reading Faustus as a mouthpiece for what is taken to be Marlowe's fraught intellectualising (see Author and Works). Nicholas Brooke's original analysis ('The Moral Tragedy of *Dr Faustus*', *Cambridge Journal* V (1951–2), reprinted in Jump, pp. 101–33) breaks out of this pattern in ways which foreshadow **postmodern** approaches to literature. Brooke sees Faustus as challenging the Manichaean universe in which the equal but opposite Devil and God confront each other. Faustus's project is to create himself as another god, an ambition which is licensed by the theological premise that man, being made in God's image, contains god-like aspirations. It is thus natural, even in-built, that Faustus should contain the possibility of being a deity, and correspondingly unjust that God should forbid him from developing that possibility. To break out of the God-dominated world, Faustus must exert resolution: the absolute will-power to keep himself (in his own mind) a separate entity, and judged by his own morality. Faustus loses his battle – and his virtue – precisely at those moments when he thinks of repentance and his resolution falters. This is a complete reversal of the usual interpretation that such moments bring him closer to salvation.

The status of the comic scenes has also received varying opinions. One position is to find them so unfunny that they require explaining away, either as feeble interpolations, or as simple indications that Faustus is becoming degraded by his devilish pastimes. Those critics most alive to performance possibilities, however, see them as an integral part of the play's effect (see also Structure). D.J. Palmer ('Magic and Poetry in *Dr Faustus*', *Critical Quarterly* VI (1964), reprinted in Jump, pp. 188–203) influentially sees coherences between the 'comic' scenes of trickery and the 'serious' scenes, where the devils' shows and fakes are crucial to Faustus's decision-making. He then concludes that the play is **self-referential**: it is about 'the magic of stage illusion'. Such a theory is very persuasive, especially in relation to performance criticism (see Recent Criticism).

Textual scholars have dealt at great length with the problems of authenticity raised by the existence of the A-text and the (longer) B-text: see Note on the Text for detailed comment on this matter.

RECENT CRITICISM

Although there is often a certain amount of overlap, a number of more or less distinct schools of thought can be identified in contemporary approaches to *Doctor Faustus*.

PERFORMANCE CRITICISM

In performance criticism, the printed play text that is normally read and studied is seen as an incomplete blueprint for an imagined complete form, which, in turn, is achieved in performance. According to this theory a play is thus ephemeral: a highly fluid object of study that vanishes in taking place. Each production is different from every other, and if one adds the concept of rapport with the audience to the definition of a play, each *performance* is a unique event, different from every other. Performance criticism thus reads the *staging* of a play for its meaning, and not just the text. One needs to consider the effect of casting, costume, style and so forth as part of a meaningful system of signs. Parts of the discussion of Characterisation and the critical commentaries on the Detailed Summaries in this Note lead towards a performance-based approach to *Doctor Faustus*.

Performance criticism also draws on theories of **carnival**, and consequently intersects with both New Historicism and (via its concern with the body) psychoanalytic criticism (see below). Carnival is to do with participation in normally unacceptable behaviour – blocking streets, making fun of authority and so on – on specially allocated days. It is simultaneously both subversive and controlled, and is thus a licensed forum where authority can be **satirised.** In some circumstances such satire can become a new basis of power amongst the people, and so lead to revolution. In other circumstances carnival allows oppressed groups to 'let off steam', after which the accustomed hierarchy returns; in such cases it becomes a device to keep exploited or less powerful groups in society contented, and functions as a conservative rather than a revolutionary mode.

There are clear implications of theories of carnival for the main plot of *Doctor Faustus*, where rebellion against (divine) authority takes place. When Faustus's carnivalesque behaviour goes beyond theologically licensed bounds, it is quelled. The critical concept of carnival is even more relevant to the **low comic** scenes, since it enables a **parodic** reading of those scenes, and theorises their incorporation into *Doctor Faustus* as the voice of an alternative judgement (see also Structure). It is up to performance to make such a reading clear to an audience, challenging those who regard the comic scenes as inferior and irrelevant.

NEW HISTORICISM

New Historicism is concerned with the ways in which power structures in society are represented in society's literary (and other artistic) products. Further, it is concerned with the ways in which such representations are manipulated in order to reinforce power structures and images of society through the symbolic codes of display. Based on the work of the French critic Roland Barthes and developed by many others, notably Stephen Greenblatt, New Historicism recounts ways in which literature is not 'innocent' or neutral, but politicised and committed to certain, often unspoken, values.

Theatre is of especial interest as it involves the presentation of literary texts simultaneously with a visual display, and both of these in a medium (the production) which changes radically from one period of history to another. Stephen Greenblatt ('Marlowe and the Will to Absolute Play', in *Renaissance Self-Fashioning*, Chicago University Press, 1980) introduced the concept of 'self-fashioning' – i.e. creating an identity (in language) – using in part a discussion of Faustus. Simon Shepherd, in *Marlowe and the Politics of Elizabethan Theatre* (Harvester, Brighton, 1986), analyses *Doctor Faustus* from the point of view of its relations to power structures and cultural anxieties of the period, seeing connections between the play and subversive political thought, in particular puritanism and its concept of free speech (see Historical Background). He also considers ways in which the identity of Faustus is created on the stage by a combination of the words of the text and the actor presenting those words. Some of the preoccupations of traditional criticism (see Conventional Approaches) reappear in New Historicism, but with a different perspective. George Geckle, for example, agrees with the familiar view that individual responsibility and its consequences are worked through in *Doctor Faustus*, but takes this further ('The 1604 and 1616 Versions of *Dr Faustus*', in David Allen and Robert White (eds), *Subjects on the World's Stage: Essays in British Literature of the Middle Ages and Renaissance*, University of Delaware Press, 1995). Using a performance-based approach, Geckle sees the play as manifesting unresolved conflicts within Elizabethan society between a medieval theology (where external forces act upon a passive human subject) and a Renaissance humanism which, verging on atheism, makes individuals fully responsible for their choices (see Historical Background).

Psychoanalytic criticism

Early psychoanalytic criticism involved naïve attempts to 'read' the motivations and compulsions of literary characters as if they were real people. By extension, literary characters were sometimes treated as a means of access to the author's (presumed) psychological condition. Discussions of *Doctor Faustus* have insistently returned to psychoanalytic themes, locating traces of the Oedipus complex or **solipsistic** thinking, among other clinical matters; see, for example, Kuriyama, *Hammer or Anvil: Psychological Patterns in Christopher Marlowe's Plays* (Rutgers UP, 1980). More recent material offers insight into Faustus's concerns with physicality, dismemberment and the body.

One aspect of psychoanalytic literary criticism, following the ideas of the French thinker Jacques Lacan, deals with the relationship between identity, language and desire. According to Lacanian psychoanalytic criticism, both language and desire are functions of lack. Lack is considered to be the absence of the object of desire. A Lacanian reading of *Doctor Faustus* might, for example, show that Faustus constitutes himself as a desiring subject in his opening monologue. He lists his achievements, but finds them unsatisfactory. They fail to fill the emptiness which constitutes his identity, and he turns again and again to further, more rarefied knowledge, until only magic is left unexplored. His desire is expressed as excitement at the promised future that he anticipates (Scene 1, lines 53–5):

> O what a world of profit and delight
> Of power, of honour, or omnipotence
> Is promised to the studious artisan!

Much of what the Devil has to offer, however, is regarded as a series of linguistic substitutes for that which Faustus lacks. Both the fake apparitions and the glamorous language can be seen as 'empty' objects, since Faustus uses them as substitutes for a reality which is not present.

DECONSTRUCTION

With its hesitations and irresolutions, and its conflict between opposed belief systems (which may turn out not to be opposed at all), *Doctor Faustus* seems a natural text to draw the attention of **deconstructionist** literary critics – followers of the French thinker Jacques Derrida. The themes of the play map closely onto Derrida's major concerns: the nature of meaning; the (un)reliability of language; the insubstantiality of representation. Another Derridean concern is the repetitive recurrence of spectral figures in our lives, an issue which arises for Faustus in the form of the Good and Evil Angels, as well as in the various conjured apparitions.

As Catherine Belsey puts it (in *Critical Practice*, second edition, Routledge, 1988), *Doctor Faustus* is an 'interrogative text' that 'refuses a single point of view': the same features that open this text to a **carnivalesque** reading (see Performance Criticism) also suggest deconstruction. Jonathan Dollimore (in *Radical Tragedy*, Harvester, Brighton, 1984) agrees, perceiving that although *Doctor Faustus* involves a discovery of limits, these do not shut down subversive questioning, but in fact provoke it. Thus to a deconstructionist, *Doctor Faustus* is a plural or *scriptible* text, which endlessly renews itself in different forms the more it is read.

OTHER EDITIONS

David Bevington & Eric Rasmussen (eds), *Doctor Faustus: A- and B-Texts (1604, 1616): Christopher Marlowe and his Collaborator and Revisers*, The Revels Plays, Manchester University Press, 1993
> The thorough introduction addresses many of the issues raised in this Note

J.B. Steane (ed.), *Christopher Marlowe: The Complete Plays*, Penguin, 1969
> The introduction (pp. 22–7) offers a clear discussion of the B-text of *Doctor Faustus* which follows traditional patterns of criticism (see Conventional Approaches)

BIOGRAPHY

Leslie Hotson, *The Death of Christopher Marlowe*, Nonesuch Press, London, 1925
> This was the first really thorough piece of scholarship to cast doubt on the official account of Christopher Marlowe's death

Charles Nicoll, *The Reckoning: The Murder of Christopher Marlowe*, Jonathan Cape, 1992
> A very readable description of Marlowe's London lifestyle, and of the people with whom he associated. Nicoll argues that Marlowe was murdered for political reasons

CRITICISM

The history of critical responses to *Doctor Faustus* is discussed by Roma Gill in the introduction to the selected text (New Mermaids second edition, A & C Black/W.W. Norton, 1989, reprinted 1994).

Collections of critical essays on *Doctor Faustus* and Christopher Marlowe can be found in John D. Jump (ed.), *Marlowe: Doctor Faustus*, Casebook Series (Macmillan, 1969); Clifford Leech (ed.), *Marlowe: A Collection of Critical Essays* (Prentice-Hall, 1964); and Judith O'Neil (ed.), *Critics on Marlowe* (University of Miami Press, 1969).

In addition to the texts mentioned in the Conventional Approaches and Recent Criticism sections, the following present a range of approaches to *Doctor Faustus*:

Donald Cole, *Suffering and Evil in the Plays of Christopher Marlowe*, Princeton UP, 1962
Considers aspects of suffering and evil in relation to *Doctor Faustus*, as well as Marlowe's other plays

Michael Hattaway, *Elizabethan Popular Theatre: Plays in Performance*, Routledge & Kegan Paul, 1982
Contains a section on performances of *Doctor Faustus*

Jan Kott (translated by D. Miedzyrzecka & L. Valle), *The Bottom Translation: Marlowe and Shakespeare and the Carnival Tradition*, Northwestern University Press, Evanston, Illinois, 1987
Uses the theory of carnival in conjunction with performance-based readings

Harry Levin, *Christopher Marlowe: The Overreacher*, Faber & Faber, 1967
Discusses Christopher Marlowe's use of language

William Tydeman, *Doctor Faustus: Text and Performance*, Macmillan, 1984
Illuminates the variety of performance possibilities in *Doctor Faustus*

Elizabeth Wright, *Psychoanalytic Criticism: Theory in Practice*, Methuen, 1984
Using readily comprehended language, Wright shows ways in which psychoanalysis can be relevant to reading literary texts

World events	Marlowe's life	Literature/drama
c1448 Birth of Georgius Faustus, the man on whom Marlowe's protagonist was based		
		1516 Thomas More writes Latin work *Utopia*
1519 Charles V becomes Holy Roman Emperor		
1527 Birth of future King Philip II of Spain, son of Charles V		**1527** John Colet's *Aeditio* is published posthumously
1530 Martin Luther and others compose the Augsburg Confession, marking the culmination of the German Reformation		
1533 Birth of future Queen Elizabeth I of England		
		1534 Publication of Martin Luther's German translation of the Bible
1535 Execution of Sir Thomas More		**1535** First complete English translation of the Bible (by Miles Coverdale) is published
1536 Death of Desiderius Erasmus, Dutch priest and humanist thinker		
c1541 Death of Georgius Faustus		
1546 Death of Martin Luther		
		1551 Ralph Robynson translates More's *Utopia* into English
1553 Mary I becomes Queen of England		
1554 Mary I of England marries Philip II of Spain		
1556 Charles V abdicates, dividing his empire between Philip II of Spain and brother Ferdinand I of Austria		
1558 Elizabeth I accedes to the English throne following death of Mary I; death of former Charles V; birth of Thomas Kyd		
1564 Birth of William Shakespeare	**1564** Birth of Christopher Marlowe at Canterbury	
1566 Birth of Edward Alleyn		
1568 Mary, Queen of Scots imprisoned by Elizabeth I		**1568** Richard Grafton, *A Chronicle at Large of the Affairs of England from the Creation of the World unto the First Year of Queen Elizabeth*
		1569 Edmund Spenser, *The Visions of Bellay* and *The Visions of Petrarch*

World events	Marlowe's life	Literature/drama
1573 Sir Francis Walsingham appointed Secretary of State		
1576 James Burbage erects the first permanent theatre in England since Roman times		
	1579 Obtains scholarship to study at the King's School, Canterbury	
	1580-7 Studies at Corpus Christi College, Cambridge University; visits France in the mid-1580s probably working for Sir Francis Walsingham's secret service; is awarded BA degree in 1584; probably writes *Dido, Queen of Carthage* whilst at Cambridge	
1584-5 Sir Walter Raleigh's expedition fails to colonise Virginia		
1587 Mary, Queen of Scots executed after being implicated in plot to murder Elizabeth I; financier Philip Henslowe opens the Rose Theatre, where Alleyn leads performances of several of Marlowe's plays	**1587** After receiving MA from Cambridge, Marlowe moves to London and begins writing plays for Lord Strange's Men and for Pembroke's company; first performance of *Tamburlaine the Great* – a huge success; later that year *Tamburlaine the Great, Part II* is performed	**1587** Thomas Kyd writes *The Spanish Tragedy*
1588 Philip II initiates war with England, which continues despite England's defeat of the Spanish Armada	**c1588** Probable earliest performance of *Doctor Faustus* at the Belsavage playhouse	
	1589 Marlowe arrested on a murder charge but is released after 13 days in Newgate Prison; writes *The Jew of Malta* around this time	**1589** Thomas Nashe, *The Anatomy of Absurdity*
1590 Death of Sir Francis Walsingham	**1590** Publication of *Tamburlaine the Great*, the only one of Marlowe's works to be published during his lifetime	**1590** Thomas Watson, *Eclogue upon the Death of Sir Francis Walsingham*; Edmund Spenser starts *The Faerie Queene* (Books I–III)
		c1590-2 William Shakespeare writes his first plays, including Parts I–III of *Henry VI*
	c1591-3 First performances of *Edward II*	
1592 Edward Alleyn marries Henslowe's stepdaughter	**1592** Bound over to keep the peace following a brawl	**1592** Orwin's translation of the German *Faustbuch* printed (probably not the first edition); Kyd's *The Spanish Tragedy* is published anonymously
1592-4 Theatres in London closed due to outbreak of the plague		

World events	Marlowe's life	Literature/drama
	1593 First performance of *The Massacre at Paris*, at the Rose Theatre; Christopher Marlowe is called before the Privy Council, and later the same month is stabbed to death in Deptford	
1594 Death of Thomas Kyd		**1594** Shakespeare, *Titus Andronicus*; Thomas Kyd, *Cornelia*
1595 Sir Walter Raleigh sails to Guyana in search of El Dorado		
		1596 Edmund Spenser completes all six books of *The Faerie Queene*; Sir Walter Raleigh publishes his *The Discovery of the Empire of Guiana*
		1596-8 First performances of Shakespeare's *The Merchant of Venice*
1598 Death of Philip II of Spain	**1598** Marlowe's *Hero and Leander* is published posthumously	
		1599 Shakespeare, *Henry V*
1600 The Fortune Theatre is built for Henslowe and Alleyn		
	1601 The play of *Doctor Faustus* is entered in the Stationers' Register	
	1602 Alterations to *Doctor Faustus* commissioned by Philip Henslowe	
1603 Death of Elizabeth I; James Stuart accedes to the throne		
1604 War between England and Spain ends	**1604** Publication of the A-text of *Doctor Faustus*	
1605 Discovery of the Gunpowder Plot to blow up the English Parliament – Guy Fawkes arrested		**1605** Shakespeare, *King Lear*; Cervantes, *Don Quixote de la Mancha* (Part I); Ben Jonson, *The Masque of Blackness* (produced in collaboration with Inigo Jones)
1606 The Act of Abuses bans the naming of God on stage		
		1610 John Donne, *Pseudo-Martyr*
		1614 John Webster, *The Duchess of Malfi*
		1615 Cervantes, *Don Quixote de la Mancha* (Part II)
1616 Death of William Shakespeare	**1616** Publication of the B-text of *Doctor Faustus*	
1618 Death of Sir Walter Raleigh		
1626 Death of Edward Alleyn		

allegory a figurative representation within a narrative of abstract concepts by characters bearing their names (for example in the parade of the Seven Deadly Sins in Scene 5 of *Doctor Faustus*). An allegory is thus an extended metaphor or a sustained personification

alliteration a sequence of repeated consonantal sounds in a stretch of written or spoken text. The matching consonants are usually at the beginning of words or stressed syllables

ambivalence the co-existence of two different (and usually opposed) attitudes towards the same thing

aporia (Greek: 'impassable path') a word used in rhetoric for the pondering of a difficult question. More specifically, the term is used in the theory of deconstruction to refer to that point in all discourses at which some internal contradiction or irresolvable paradox betrays the instability of meaning, an instability which is regarded as the condition of all language

argument a logically reasoned construction in which premisses are analysed to arrive at a conclusion. The validity of an argument has nothing to do with its truth, since that depends on the accuracy of the premisses on which the argument's conclusion is based

ballad rhythm (ballad metre) a four-lined stanza of alternate four-stress and three-stress lines, usually roughly iambic

bathos (Greek: 'depth') a ludicrous descent from the elevated treatment of a subject to the dull and trivial

blank verse unrhymed iambic pentameter

Brechtian following the theories, styles and stage techniques of the German playwright Bertolt Brecht (1898–1956). Brecht advocated the use of anti-realistic devices to maintain an audience's awareness of the fact that they are watching a representation of reality, not reality itself; this technique became known as the 'alienation effect'

carnival a literary phenomenon described by the Russian critic Mikhail Bakhtin (1895–1975), especially in his work *Rabelais and his World* (tr. Hélène Iswolsky, Cambridge, MA & London, 1968; first published in Russian, 1965). According to Bakhtin, some writers use their works as an outlet for the spirit of carnival, of popular festivity and misrule. They 'subvert' the literary culture of the ruling classes, undermining its claim to moral monopoly. Such forms and genres are open and 'dialogic': they allow multiple points of view to co-exist and are valued for their availability to plural interpretations. See also Michael Bristol, *Carnival and Theater: Plebeian Culture and the Structure of Authority* (Methuen, 1985) for further useful explanation of this important critical concept

closure the sense of completeness and finality achieved by the endings of some literary works (or parts of literary works)

convention a standard, common feature of a particular genre of literature (or a set of such features). Recurring elements in all kinds of literature, whether of technique or subject matter, turn into the conventions of that form which new authors may copy, alter or reject

couplet a pair of consecutive lines of poetry which rhyme together

deconstruction most of the ideas of the theory of deconstruction originate in the complex works of the French philosopher Jacques Derrida (b. 1930). He believes that all notions of the existence of an absolute meaning in language are wrong; yet this assumption has dominated Western thought, and it should be the aim of the philosopher and critic, Derrida argues, to 'deconstruct' the philosophy and literature of the past to expose this false assumption and reveal the essential paradox at the heart of language. To 'deconstruct' a text is merely to show how texts deconstruct themselves because of this fundamental indeterminateness at the core of language – one reason for the difficulty of Derrida's own writing is that he is aware of his own texts deconstructing themselves. The word 'deconstruction' is now often used merely to refer to the revelation of partially hidden meanings in a text, especially those that illuminate aspects of its relationship with its social and political context. In its weakest form, 'deconstruct' has become a jargon word for 'analyse' or 'interpret'

decorum the tradition of using particular verse forms and kinds of diction for particular circumstances. It can be thought of as a sense of the appropriate

dénouement (French: 'unknotting') the final unfolding of a plot: the point at which the audience's or reader's expectations, be they hopes or fears, about what will happen to the characters are finally satisfied or denied

despair in the Early Modern period, 'despair' meant loss of faith in God, and was signified by suicide; the two were often treated as synonymous

dialogue generally, the speech and conversation of characters in any kind of literary work; the term is also used to denote a specific form of logical reasoning, and genre of literature, consisting of a discussion between characters. Plato's dialogues of Socrates (fourth century BC) are amongst the earliest and most famous examples of the dialogue genre

diction a general term used to describe the kind of vocabulary used in a work of literature

dramatic irony a feature of a play whereby the development of the plot allows the audience more information about what is happening than some of the characters themselves have

dumb show a mimed representation of the narrative of the main play. The best-known examples are the mime that precedes the play of 'The Mouse-trap' in Shakespeare's *Hamlet*, and the dumb shows in John Webster's *The White Devil* (1612)

elegy a poem of lamentation, concentrating on the death of a single person

elements the four elements of medieval science, medicine and philosophy: earth, air, water and fire. They were part of a complex system of correspondences in which every part of the natural world had an affiliation to one of them, or to a combination of them. They are related to the system of the humours, which supposedly governed personality and somatic types

end-stopped an end-stopped line of verse is one in which the end of the line coincides with the conclusion of a sentence, or the strongly-marked end of a phrase (usually signalled by punctuation). An end-stopped line thus creates a sense of finality and allows the possibility of a minute pause before the next line is delivered. Christopher Marlowe does not use this style invariably – he also makes use of enjambment

enjambment (French: *enjambement* 'straddling') the practice of running one line of verse into the next syntactically, such that they are spoken with no break between them

episodic denoting a narrative which is written in the simple form of a series of more or less separable or discrete episodes or incidents, rather than a complicated or involved plot

epyllion (Greek: 'little epic poem') a short narrative poem or 'brief epic', in fashion throughout the 1590s

form the conventional pattern or shape which one expects each example of a genre to possess in order to classify it as part of that genre. Any repeated element will give a sense of pattern which can be considered an aspect of form

generalisation a claim, theory or principle with general application, often manifested in the form of a large and all-encompassing statement. To generalise is to utter truths which apply to all relevant cases. It is usually difficult to generalise adequately and validly on any subject, and so the word has acquired a common pejorative force: to say that a statement is 'just a generalisation' is to imply that it is untrue in many of the cases in which it is supposed to apply

heroic couplet a pair of rhyming lines in iambic pentameter

homily a sermon-like discourse (whether spoken or written) or short lecture intended to be morally edifying

hubris (Greek: 'pride, arrogance') the self-indulgent confidence that causes a tragic hero to ignore the decrees, laws and warnings of the gods, and therefore defy them to bring about his or her downfall

humours in ancient medical theory, lasting till the seventeenth century, there were supposed to be four principal 'humours' in the human body: phlegm, blood, choler and black bile. If any one of these predominated in a person's constitution, then that individual's character would be phlegmatic, sanguine, choleric or melancholic. The humours were conceived as part of an elaborate system in which the qualities of moist, dry, hot and cold related to the elements, to colours, and also to herbs and plants; all these were also related to the humours

hyperbole (Greek: 'throwing too far') emphasis by exaggeration; hyperbolic language is common in everyday speech and in all kinds of literature

iamb the commonest metrical foot in English verse, consisting of an unstressed syllable followed by a stressed syllable

iambic pentameter a line of verse containing five iambs

imagery in its narrowest sense an image is a picture in words – a description of some visible scene or object. More commonly, however, 'imagery' refers to the figurative language in a work of literature; or all the words which refer to objects and qualities which appeal to the senses and feelings

implicit suggested but not expressed outright in the 'literal' sense of the words used

in medias res (Latin: 'into the middle of things') a phrase describing a common technique of storytelling in which the narrator begins not at the beginning of a story or action, but in the middle

irony a use of language, widespread in all kinds of literature and everyday speech, which is characterised by saying or writing one thing while another is meant; irony that is overdone rather than understated becomes sarcasm. Ironic statements in literature are not always easily discerned or understood; in certain cases the context of an ironic comment will make clear the actual meaning intended, but more often a writer will have to rely on the reader's shared knowledge and values

low comedy unlike high comedy, which appeals to the intellect, low comedy is aimed at provoking unthinking laughter by the simplest of means – physical action, such as violent or slapstick horseplay, ribald jokes, clowning and ridiculous clothes are all common in low comedy on the stage. Low comedy may also include comedy by 'lower' social classes, following the principle of decorum. Wagner's intellectual playfulness may be seen as low comedy for two reasons: firstly because he is a servant (and hence from a 'lower' social class); and secondly because his cheeky verbal style has a random, knockabout quality reminiscent of the disruptions involved in physical slapstick

mankind figure the central character in a Morality Play, representative of the ordinary human existence of each of us

metaphor (Greek: 'carrying over') a departure from literal writing which goes further than a comparison between two different things or ideas by fusing them together: one thing is described as being another thing, thus 'carrying over' all its associations

Morality Play an allegory in which the forces of good and evil and a Christian moral lesson concerning salvation are dramatised with simplicity and vigour. Many Morality Plays contained a character called the Vice, a half-comic, half-evil tempter (see Literary Background)

Mystery Play (Latin: *misterium*, from *ministerium* 'handicraft, guild') a dramatisation of the Old and New Testaments. Mystery Plays evolved steadily from about the tenth century onwards, and by the fourteenth century elaborate cycles had developed, which were played in summer during the feast of Corpus Christi, with each guild responsible for a biblical episode. Each scene was presented on a waggon which could be moved around the city. The verse tends to be rough and vigorous, but the later plays show a strong sense of character and psychology

paradox an apparently self-contradictory statement or one that seems to be in conflict with all logic and opinion; yet lying behind the superficial absurdity is a meaning or truth

parody an imitation of a specific work of literature or style, devised so as to ridicule its characteristic features

personification a variety of figurative or metaphoric language in which things or ideas are treated as if they were human beings, with human attributes and feelings

phenomenon an object or occurrence perceived by the senses

playwright a creator of play texts. The form of the second part of the word, 'wright', indicates that a play is 'made' as much as it is written

polysyllable a word consisting of three or more syllables

postmodernism a term originally used to describe a movement and tendency in all the arts – and in culture in general – coming after (and usually in reaction to) modernism, 'postmodernism' has become a somewhat vague concept of disputed meaning and value. As it relates to thinking about language, postmodernism can be regarded as denoting a mode of discussion which develops the insight that meaning is not inherent in language, but is 'constructed' by conventional frameworks of thought. Things (including words), therefore, are empty of meaning until the culture which uses them invests them with significance

prolepsis (Greek: 'anticipation, taking before') the anticipation of future events in a narrative. In rhetoric, the pre-emptive technique in which objections are anticipated and answered in advance is termed 'proleptic'

prose any language that is not patterned by the regularity of some kind of metre. It is contrasted with verse, which contains some element of repetition (for example in the use of rhythm or rhyme), creating a pattern

quarto (Latin: *in quarto* 'in quarter') a paper and book size: a printer's sheet is folded twice to make four leaves (eight pages)

rhetoric (Greek: *rhetor* 'public speaker') the art of speaking (and writing) effectively so as to persuade an audience. Rhetoric was the subject of several textbooks by Greek and Roman scholars, including Aristotle and Cicero, and was studied at universities during the Middle Ages and the Renaissance

rhetorical question a question asked not for the sake of enquiry but for emphasis: the writer or speaker expects the reader or audience to be totally convinced about the appropriate reply

rhyme though by no means all verse is rhymed (for example, much of *Doctor Faustus* is written in blank verse), rhyme is one of the most striking and obvious differences between verse and prose, and the most easily identified common aspect of English versification. It consists of chiming or matching sounds at the ends of lines of verse, which create a very clearly audible sense of pattern. *Doctor Faustus* contains many examples of 'near rhyme', where the matching of final sounds is audible but not quite perfectly identical, as in lines 27–8 of the Prologue:

> Which he prefers before his chiefest bliss.
> And this the man that in his study sits.

The ends of these two lines share the same vowel sound ('i') and the same consonant ('s') but in the second line the sound 't' intervenes between the two

satire literature which exhibits or examines vice and folly and makes them appear ridiculous or contemptible. Satire is directed against a person or a type, and is usually morally censorious, using laughter as a means of attack rather than merely for the evocation of mirth or pleasure

scriptible (French: 'writable, writerly') the term was used by the French critic Roland Barthes (1915–80) to indicate a special kind of complex, open-ended text that requires the reader's constant and active participation in order to be comprehensible. This is contrasted with the '*lisible*' ('readable, readerly') text, which can be read in a passive and inert way

self-referential and **self-reflexive** terms describing a text that refers to itself – for example, a text in which the writer discusses the processes of composition, or in which the content of the text addresses the nature of the creative genre to which it belongs

soliloquy (Latin: *soliloquium* 'speaking alone') a dramatic convention which allows a character in a play to speak directly to the audience, as if thinking aloud about motives, feelings and decisions. Part of the convention is that a soliloquy provides accurate access to the character's innermost thoughts: we perhaps learn more about the character in this way than could ever be gathered from the action of the play alone

solipsism a philosophical theory postulating that nothing exists except the self

sonnet a lyric poem of fixed form: fourteen lines of iambic pentameter rhymed and organised according to one of a number of intricate schemes

stichomythia (Greek: *stikhomuthein* 'to speak alternate lines') a form of dialogue in which speakers alternate, each speaker having one line at a time

syllogism a mathematically precise method of argument in logic, in which one proposition (the conclusion) may be reached by deductive inference from two others (the premisses). A syllogism may be valid or invalid, but cannot be true or false

symbol something which represents something else (often an idea or quality) by analogy or association – a writer may use conventional symbols, which form part of a literary or cultural tradition, as well as creating new ones

theatre-in-the-round theatre arranged so as to allow the audience to surround the actors on all sides (instead of the normal confrontation between players and audience)

theme the abstract subject of a work; its central idea or ideas, which may or may not be explicit or obvious. A text may contain several themes or thematic interests

topos (Greek: 'place') a common or recurrent motif in literature

tragedy one of the most discussed genres in literature; a tragedy traces the career and downfall of an individual and shows in this downfall – which is typically due to a single flaw in the individual's character – both the capacities and the limitations of human life. The protagonist may be superhuman, a monarch, or, in the modern age, an ordinary person. In English literature the Elizabethan and Jacobean periods constitute the great age of tragedy

Vice the principal tempter and agent of the Devil in a Morality Play. His stage business includes changing his name, making plots and lying, cowardice and beating his followers with a wooden sword or dagger

vice-crew a group of two or three followers of the Vice. Their stage business includes great stupidity, noisy roaring and singing part-songs ('Three Men's Songs')

Author of this note

Jill Barker completed her first degree at the Australian National University, before taking an MA and a PhD at the University of Warwick. After a career in progressive secondary education, she is now a Senior Lecturer in the Department of Literary Studies at the University of Luton, with special interests in feminist and psychoanalytic interpretations of sixteenth-century literature. Her published work includes reviews of editions of Shakespeare for *The Year's Work in English Studies*, book chapters on psychoanalytic literary theory, and articles on the representation of women in Shakespeare.

NOTES

York Notes Advanced (£3.99 each)

Margaret Atwood
The Handmaid's Tale

Jane Austen
Mansfield Park

Jane Austen
Persuasion

Jane Austen
Pride and Prejudice

Alan Bennett
Talking Heads

William Blake
*Songs of Innocence and of
Experience*

Charlotte Brontë
Jane Eyre

Emily Brontë
Wuthering Heights

Geoffrey Chaucer
The Franklin's Tale

Geoffrey Chaucer
*General Prologue to the
Canterbury Tales*

Geoffrey Chaucer
*The Wife of Bath's Prologue
and Tale*

Joseph Conrad
Heart of Darkness

Charles Dickens
Great Expectations

John Donne
Selected Poems

George Eliot
The Mill on the Floss

F. Scott Fitzgerald
The Great Gatsby

E.M. Forster
A Passage to India

Brian Friel
Translations

Thomas Hardy
The Mayor of Casterbridge

Thomas Hardy
Tess of the d'Urbervilles

Seamus Heaney
*Selected Poems from Opened
Ground*

Nathaniel Hawthorne
The Scarlet Letter

James Joyce
Dubliners

John Keats
Selected Poems

Christopher Marlowe
Doctor Faustus

Arthur Miller
Death of a Salesman

Toni Morrison
Beloved

William Shakespeare
Antony and Cleopatra

William Shakespeare
As You Like It

William Shakespeare
Hamlet

William Shakespeare
King Lear

William Shakespeare
Measure for Measure

William Shakespeare
The Merchant of Venice

William Shakespeare
Much Ado About Nothing

William Shakespeare
Othello

William Shakespeare
Romeo and Juliet

William Shakespeare
The Tempest

William Shakespeare
The Winter's Tale

Mary Shelley
Frankenstein

Alice Walker
The Color Purple

Oscar Wilde
*The Importance of Being
Earnest*

Tennessee Williams
A Streetcar Named Desire

John Webster
The Duchess of Malfi

W.B. Yeats
Selected Poems

GCSE and equivalent levels (£3.50 each)

Maya Angelou
I Know Why the Caged Bird Sings

Jane Austen
Pride and Prejudice

Alan Ayckbourn
Absent Friends

Elizabeth Barrett Browning
Selected Poems

Robert Bolt
A Man for All Seasons

Harold Brighouse
Hobson's Choice

Charlotte Brontë
Jane Eyre

Emily Brontë
Wuthering Heights

Shelagh Delaney
A Taste of Honey

Charles Dickens
David Copperfield

Charles Dickens
Great Expectations

Charles Dickens
Hard Times

Charles Dickens
Oliver Twist

Roddy Doyle
Paddy Clarke Ha Ha Ha

George Eliot
Silas Marner

George Eliot
The Mill on the Floss

William Golding
Lord of the Flies

Oliver Goldsmith
She Stoops To Conquer

Willis Hall
The Long and the Short and the Tall

Thomas Hardy
Far from the Madding Crowd

Thomas Hardy
The Mayor of Casterbridge

Thomas Hardy
Tess of the d'Urbervilles

Thomas Hardy
The Withered Arm and other Wessex Tales

L.P. Hartley
The Go-Between

Seamus Heaney
Selected Poems

Susan Hill
I'm the King of the Castle

Barry Hines
A Kestrel for a Knave

Louise Lawrence
Children of the Dust

Harper Lee
To Kill a Mockingbird

Laurie Lee
Cider with Rosie

Arthur Miller
The Crucible

Arthur Miller
A View from the Bridge

Robert O'Brien
Z for Zachariah

Frank O'Connor
My Oedipus Complex and other stories

George Orwell
Animal Farm

J.B. Priestley
An Inspector Calls

Willy Russell
Educating Rita

Willy Russell
Our Day Out

J.D. Salinger
The Catcher in the Rye

William Shakespeare
Henry IV Part 1

William Shakespeare
Henry V

William Shakespeare
Julius Caesar

William Shakespeare
Macbeth

William Shakespeare
The Merchant of Venice

William Shakespeare
A Midsummer Night's Dream

William Shakespeare
Much Ado About Nothing

William Shakespeare
Romeo and Juliet

William Shakespeare
The Tempest

William Shakespeare
Twelfth Night

George Bernard Shaw
Pygmalion

Mary Shelley
Frankenstein

R.C. Sherriff
Journey's End

Rukshana Smith
Salt on the snow

John Steinbeck
Of Mice and Men

Robert Louis Stevenson
Dr Jekyll and Mr Hyde

Jonathan Swift
Gulliver's Travels

Robert Swindells
Daz 4 Zoe

Mildred D. Taylor
Roll of Thunder, Hear My Cry

Mark Twain
Huckleberry Finn

James Watson
Talking in Whispers

William Wordsworth
Selected Poems

A Choice of Poets

Mystery Stories of the Nineteenth Century including The Signalman

Nineteenth Century Short Stories

Poetry of the First World War

Six Women Poets

Chinua Achebe
Things Fall Apart

Edward Albee
Who's Afraid of Virginia Woolf?

Margaret Atwood
Cat's Eye

Jane Austen
Emma

Jane Austen
Northanger Abbey

Jane Austen
Sense and Sensibility

Samuel Beckett
Waiting for Godot

Robert Browning
Selected Poems

Robert Burns
Selected Poems

Angela Carter
Nights at the Circus

Geoffrey Chaucer
The Merchant's Tale

Geoffrey Chaucer
The Miller's Tale

Geoffrey Chaucer
The Nun's Priest's Tale

Samuel Taylor Coleridge
Selected Poems

Daniel Defoe
Moll Flanders

Daniel Defoe
Robinson Crusoe

Charles Dickens
Bleak House

Charles Dickens
Hard Times

Emily Dickinson
Selected Poems

Carol Ann Duffy
Selected Poems

George Eliot
Middlemarch

T.S. Eliot
The Waste Land

T.S. Eliot
Selected Poems

Henry Fielding
Joseph Andrews

E.M. Forster
Howards End

John Fowles
The French Lieutenant's Woman

Robert Frost
Selected Poems

Elizabeth Gaskell
North and South

Stella Gibbons
Cold Comfort Farm

Graham Greene
Brighton Rock

Thomas Hardy
Jude the Obscure

Thomas Hardy
Selected Poems

Joseph Heller
Catch-22

Homer
The Iliad

Homer
The Odyssey

Gerard Manley Hopkins
Selected Poems

Aldous Huxley
Brave New World

Kazuo Ishiguro
The Remains of the Day

Ben Jonson
The Alchemist

Ben Jonson
Volpone

James Joyce
A Portrait of the Artist as a Young Man

Philip Larkin
Selected Poems

D.H. Lawrence
The Rainbow

D.H. Lawrence
Selected Stories

D.H. Lawrence
Sons and Lovers

D.H. Lawrence
Women in Love

John Milton
Paradise Lost Bks I & II

John Milton
Paradise Lost Bks IV & IX

Thomas More
Utopia

Sean O'Casey
Juno and the Paycock

George Orwell
Nineteen Eighty-four

John Osborne
Look Back in Anger

Wilfred Owen
Selected Poems

Sylvia Plath
Selected Poems

Alexander Pope
Rape of the Lock and other poems

Ruth Prawer Jhabvala
Heat and Dust

Jean Rhys
Wide Sargasso Sea

William Shakespeare
As You Like It

William Shakespeare
Coriolanus

William Shakespeare
Henry IV Pt 1

William Shakespeare
Henry V

William Shakespeare
Julius Caesar

William Shakespeare
Macbeth

William Shakespeare
Measure for Measure

William Shakespeare
A Midsummer Night's Dream

William Shakespeare
Richard II

William Shakespeare
Richard III

William Shakespeare
Sonnets

William Shakespeare
The Taming of the Shrew

William Shakespeare
Twelfth Night

William Shakespeare
The Winter's Tale

George Bernard Shaw
Arms and the Man

George Bernard Shaw
Saint Joan

Muriel Spark
The Prime of Miss Jean Brodie

John Steinbeck
The Grapes of Wrath

John Steinbeck
The Pearl

Tom Stoppard
Arcadia

Tom Stoppard
*Rosencrantz and Guildenstern
are Dead*

Jonathan Swift
*Gulliver's Travels and The
Modest Proposal*

Alfred, Lord Tennyson
Selected Poems

W.M. Thackeray
Vanity Fair

Virgil
The Aeneid

Edith Wharton
The Age of Innocence

Tennessee Williams
Cat on a Hot Tin Roof

Tennessee Williams
The Glass Menagerie

Virginia Woolf
Mrs Dalloway

Virginia Woolf
To the Lighthouse

William Wordsworth
Selected Poems

Metaphysical Poets